JAMES G. FORLONG FUND

A GUIDE TO

THE ROMANIZATION

OF BURMESE

by

JOHN OKELL

Published by
THE ROYAL ASIATIC SOCIETY OF GREAT BRITAIN
AND IRELAND
and sold by its Agents
LUZAC AND COMPANY LTD.
46 Great Russell Street, London WC1B 3PE
1971

Transferred to Digital Printing 2004

SBN. 7189 0961 5

CONTENTS

1 PRELIMINARY

1.1 Introduction: scope of booklet

There is no lack of attempts at representing Burmese words in the roman alphabet, but no one system has yet been generally accepted. Writers who need to quote only a few Burmese names and the odd word usually use an ad hoc romanization which is so unsatisfactory that it can leave the Burmese-speaking reader in some doubt as to what word is intended. Writers concerned with language, on the other hand, who need to quote numerous and sometimes lengthy examples in Burmese, usually give them in a way which is accurate and consistent, but the variety of their romanizations is such that hardly any two writers use the same system, and students familiar with the writings of one have difficulty in reading the views of another.

The result of this situation is that a word romanized as *bada*, for example, could represent any one of 12 different pronunciations, each one of which could be spelled in Burmese in several different ways: one pronunciation alone has at least 72 different spelling possibilities. The disadvantages and inconvenience of the ensuing confusion (*e.g.* in library catalogues) need no stressing.

It is not the aim of this booklet to propose a new system of romanization which will solve the problem at one blow. A once-for-all solution remains, at least for a while, an unattainable ideal, for two reasons. The first is the force of habit: different groups of people—librarians, linguists, epigraphists, historians, journalists—are familiar with different kinds of romanization and find it difficult to change to a new one. However good a romanization may be, it cannot solve the problem unless everyone is willing to learn how to use it: the solution depends as much on the users as on the merits of the system. The second reason is the other side of the same coin. It is probably true that no single system can adequately answer the needs of all interested persons: though the variety of systems in use can be

1

considerably reduced, it may be impracticable to avoid using more than one system.

This booklet therefore does not set out to cure the malady, but it is offered in the hope of easing some of the symptoms. It lists and compares a number of different systems that have been used, recommending some and rejecting others, with comments on their good and bad points and on some alternative conventions. It may seem a lengthy statement for what is a relatively minor problem, but it is necessary to consider and compare as many of the available alternatives as possible in order to make out a convincing case for the few systems selected for recommendation.

It is hoped that the reference tables at the end will help students to follow more easily books that employ romanizations unfamiliar to them; and that writers on Burma and Burmese will find it convenient to say what romanization they are using by simply giving a reference to the tables, with a brief note, if necessary, of the points on which they differ. More importantly, it is hoped that some of the comments and recommendations may encourage writers to avoid the less satisfactory conventions and to adopt less widely diverging systems, so reducing the confusion that reigns at present.

1.2 Abbreviations

Apart from the usual abbreviations the following symbols are used:

+ for any symbol, Burmese or roman, to which other symbols are attached; *e.g.* ⁺, ⱦ
> to mean "becomes, is altered to, is rendered as"
∅ for "zero", *i.e.* significant absence of symbol; *e.g.* some systems have symbols for all the tones but one, so the very absence of a symbol indicates this tone: in other words its symbol is ∅

When referring to the sounds of Burmese I use a slightly modified version of Cornyn's 1958 transcription enclosed within oblique strokes, thus: /ko-nin:/. The modifications are that initial /q/ is not used, and the toneless short central vowel is shown by /ä/. This transcription, including the modifications, is set out in full in Table 5.

Books and articles are referred to by the author's name, given with the year of publication if relevant; *e.g.* Duroiselle 1916. Bibliographical details of works mentioned are listed in Section 6.

ACKNOWLEDGEMENT

I am grateful to Professor Hla Pe of London University for kindly writing out the examples in Burmese script for the press during my absence abroad in 1969.

2 THE PROBLEM

2.1 Sound and symbol: transliteration, transcription, and combined systems

One major group of difficulties in romanization arises from the fact that in Burmese, as in many languages, the *symbols* of the script do not exactly match the *sounds* of the speech.

A single symbol in the script may represent several different sounds; *e.g.*

+ ည်	= ိ	/i./	in ကြည့်	/ci./	"look"
	ေ†	/ei./	in ဖြည့်	/hpyei./	"fill"
	့	/e./	in ထည့်	/hte./	"put in"

Again, the vowel symbols represent different sounds in open and closed syllables; *e.g.*

ေ + ာ	=	/o:/	in ေတာ	/to:/	"forest"
	but	/au/	in ေတာင်	/taun/	"hill"
ို	=	/ou/	in ို	/sou/	"be wet"
	but	/ai/	in ိုက်	/sai'/	"plant"

Or a symbol may represent no sound at all; *e.g.*

+ ွယ် in ကိုယ် /kou/ "body" (= ကို /kou/)

+ ၉ in နဂို၉ /nägou/ "origin" (= နဂို /nägou/)

+ ဲ in ဗိုဲ /bou/ "leader" (= ဗို /bou/)

+ ဗ် in ဂြိုဟ် /jou/ "planet" (= ဂြို /jou/)

Conversely, a single sound in speech may be represented by several different symbols; *e.g.* the sound /d/ may be written

ဒ ဓ ၎ or ဝ

or, when tightly linked to a preceding syllable

တ ထ ၎ or ဠ

Again, what is sounded as a final glottal stop /ʔ/ may be symbolized in at least four ways:

က် စ် တ် or ပ်

and what is sounded as a nasalized vowel /+n/ is represented by

င် ဉ် ည် or မ်

and other symbols as well. Or a sound may have no particular symbol; e.g. the vowel of the first syllable in the following words, though pronounced the same in all of them (/ä/), is written differently in each:

စ နီ	/säni¹/	ဖိ ဖ ပ်	/hpäna¹/
စာ ရေး	/säyei:/	ဘီ လူး	/bälu:/
စား ပွဲ	/säbwe:/	လ ည်း ကောင်း	/lägaun:/
ဃ ရား	/hpäya:/	မ န် ကျည်း	/mäji:/
သ ခင်း	/thähkou:/	န ဿာ	/nädha/
ကာ း တို	/kädou./	တ န်း ခို း	/tägou:/

This divergence between sounds and symbols has led to two main methods of romanization: the method usually called *transliteration* aims to represent each letter and symbol of the Burmese script by a corresponding symbol in roman script, irrespective of pronunciation; while the method usually called *transcription* aims to represent the sounds of Burmese speech, irrespective of the spelling. A third method attempts to combine both transliteration and transcription, so I call it the *combined method.*

Not everyone uses the terms "transliteration" and "transcription" in the way they are used above; e.g. the *Tables* (1930 p.i) use "transliteration" for what is here called "transcription", and Duroiselle (1916 p.81) uses "transcription" for either method of romanization. However, the distinction is observed by many, and is used here for convenience.

2.2 Burmese and the roman alphabet: ways of filling the gaps

A second group of difficulties arises from the fact that there are certain symbols in the script, and certain sounds in the speech, for which there are no obvious equivalents in the roman alphabet. The script, for example, has six letters for nasal sounds:

င ည ဏ န မ ၀

while the roman alphabet has only two that can plausibly be used to represent them:

n m

Similarly the speech has fifteen different vowels and diphthongs, while the roman alphabet has only five "vowel" letters.

This makes it necessary to adapt or invent letters to supply the deficiencies of the roman alphabet. The chief ways of doing this are:

(*a*) to use roman letters to represent sounds other than those they normally stand for in familiar western languages; *e.g. k* for a final glottal stop, *h* for aspiration of plosives, nasals, etc.

(*b*) to use two roman letters for one Burmese sound or symbol; *e.g. ui, ng*

(*c*) to use roman letters with accents or other diacritics; *e.g. ñ, è*

(*d*) to use accents or diacritics on their own; *e.g.* ', -

(*e*) to use altogether new letters; *e.g.* ŋ, θ.

Different systems of romanization vary in the extent to which they make use of these devices, and this is a major cause of their diversity.

3 SURVEY OF THE THREE METHODS OF ROMAN-IZATION

3.1 Transliteration

The Burmese use for writing their language a script which is also used for Pali, and as there is a widely accepted romanization system for Pali this can be applied with fair success to transliterating Burmese. As a result there are not many variations in the different systems using the transliteration method. Such variations as do occur affect the few extra symbols which were added to the alphabet (one or two of them from Sanskrit) to cover features peculiar to Burmese.

Transliteration seems to have been first suggested by H. L. St Barbe in 1878. He proposed (p.230) "the English symbols which are now employed in every attempt at Indian transliteration." His equivalents are the same as "the transliteration adopted by the Pali Text Society for Pali", recommended by Duroiselle in 1913, and supported by Blagden in 1914. It was set out in full by Duroiselle in 1916, and used in his *Epigraphia Birmanica* in 1919.

Duroiselle's system was devised primarily for Old Burmese and is used for this purpose virtually unchanged by Luce (1932), Than Tun (1959), and Ba Shin (1962). Its application to modern Burmese prompted one or two small modifications which may be seen in Yi Yi (1960), Sprigg (1963), Bernot (1965), Okell (1965), and Whitbread (1969).

The following is an example of romanization by Duroiselle's system:

မြန် မာ နှိုင် ငံ သူတော သနှ အ သင်း ကျ၁နှယ် စ၁တ ညီး အဖွဲ.

mranmā nuinnam sutesana asan[3] gyānay cātañ[3] aphwai[1]

3.2 Transcription

Systems of transcription had no guide-line like that provided for transliteration by the Pali romanization. They are consequently much more numerous and varied. There are some sounds which they all render by the same roman letter (*e.g. k, t, p, n, m, l, h*) but there is considerable variation in the conventions for representing certain vowels, the finals, tones, and some of the initial consonants, especially the aspirates. Final nasal, for example, is rendered in different systems by

n ng ŋ ṅ ñ or ꜓

and the hush sibilant by

sh hs hy š ʃ or ꞔ

In order to try and do justice to the variety of the transcription systems they are considered here as falling into four "types", on the basis of certain sets of characteristics which the systems in each type share to a greater or lesser extent. I call the types: early, conventional, IPA, and typewritten. Most examples of the first two are unsystematic, with imperfect phonetic observation and with inconsistencies in the representation of the same sound.

Early transcriptions are characterized by the use of *o* and *i* for /w, y/ as in *shoe* for /shwei/, *miou* for /myou./, *oo* and *ee* for /u, i/ as in *shoezeegoon* for /shwei-ziːgoun/, *ts* or *ch* for /s/ as in *tsaloe* for /sälwe/, *chagaing* for /sägainː/, *s* occasionally for /th/ as in *assaywoon* for /äthe-wun/. The rendering of /ein, oun/ by *ien, oon,* and the frequent use of *r,* suggest that the writers learnt their Burmese in Arakan or used Arakanese interpreters, while *ch* for /s/ and *s* for /th/ may indicate an approach through Mon, which preserves these values even today. The occasional use of *z* for *ts* (/c/) may be a relic of the practice of Italian missionaries such as Sangermano.

This type of transcription is used for names and words in the works of Symes (1800), Crawfurd (1834), Phayre (1853), and Yule (1858). Perhaps its most complete statement is in Latter (1845), though he is not consistent throughout. Traces of the early transcription survive today in names such as

Rangoon	for	/Yan-goun/
Yandoon	for	/Nyaun-dounː/
Toungoo	for	/Taun-ngu/
Bassein	for	/Päthein/
Salween	for	/Than-lwin/

Sandoway for /Than-dwe:/
Henzada for /Hin:dhäda./
Irrawaddy for /Ei-ya-wãdi/
Alompra for /Älaun:hpäya:/
Ramree for /Yan:bye:/
Tenasserim for /Tänin:tha-yi/

Transcribed by Latter, the sample given above would probably have come out like this:

မြန်မာနိုင်ငံ သူတော်သနာအသင်း ဂျာနယ် စာတည်းအဖွဲ့,

mrammā naing-gnaṇ thŏŏtéthană athĕng: giānay tsadee: aphuậy

Conventional transcriptions. Dissatisfaction with the early type of transcription was being voiced by 1874: St Barbe (p.228) quotes Mason as having already pointed out to the Secretariat "that no recognized system was at present in force: every Government servant was at liberty to follow his own method; the result being that the English equivalents for even the commonest vernacular names were very rarely alike in two publications." St Barbe then gives a list of seven different roman spellings which he had seen for the same name:

Shwegheen   *Shwaygyen*   *Shwegyen*   *Showegyeen*
Shwaygheen *Shwayghen*   *Showegyen*

He proposed a system that was remarkably accurate, though incomplete. Phayre claims to have "generally adopted" it in his influential *History* (1883 p.9), but in fact he retains many features of the early type, notably

ts   dz for /s   z/
eng un for /in oun/
r   for /y/

Regrettably, St Barbe's suggestions were not widely taken up, and in 1883 the secretariat published its *Tables for the transliteration of Burmese.* The transcription they put forward is known as "the Government transcription", or sometimes as "the Hunterian system", though Hunter's romanizations in fact have much more in common with the early transcriptions than with that of the *Tables*; *e.g.* in his 1881 *Gazetteer* (vol.2) he writes

3.2

Mahá-ráza weng   for   /Mäha ya-zäwin/   p.298
Kyeng-dweng   for   /Hcin:dwin:/   p.291
Theebaw   for   /Thi-bo:/   p.307
etc.

The "system" of the *Tables* was an improvement on the early type, but as it failed to mark tone and ignored the distinction between aspirate and plain consonants, it left much to be desired. A word transcribed by this method as *pwe* could stand for any one of the following six possibilities:

/pwei   pwei.   pwei: hpwei   hpwei.   hpwei:/

And *Tangyi*, the Government transcription for the name of a hill, could be any one of the following 18 words:

/Tan-ji   Tan-ji.   Tan-ji: Htan-ji   Htan-ji.   Htan-ji:/
/Tan.ji   Tan.ji.   Tan.ji: Htan.ji   Htan.ji.   Htan.ji:/
/Tan:ji   Tan:ji.   Tan:ji: Htan:ji   Htan:ji.   Htan:ji:/

The *Tables* were reissued, virtually unchanged, in 1890, 1907, and 1930. To this day they form the basis for the everyday transcription of the great majority of place-names and personal names by Burmans and foreigners alike (*e.g.* Butwell 1963, Nash 1965). It is a pity that so defective a system should have acquired such widespread use and become so firmly established.

Around the turn of the century, however, the needs of language teaching led to a more accurate recognition of the sounds distinguished in Burmese, and to the development of unambiguous ways of representing them. This type of transcription is based on the nearest likely English spellings and so bears some resemblance to the "system" of the official *Tables*, though it lacks its major defects. One of its characteristic features is the use of *t* or *k* for final glottal stop, and *n* or *ng* for final nasal. Perhaps the best example of this type is the system used by Grant Brown (1910), a modified version of which was adopted by the Library of Congress for its catalogue in 1966, and, with some small further modifications, for the library of the School of Oriental and African Studies of London University in 1967. Similar systems were used by Taw Sein Ko (1898) and Bridges (1906 etc.), though these two use a form of transliteration for the vowels.

In the original form of Grant Brown's transcription the example would be:

မြန်မာနိုင်ငံ သူတော သာ အာသင်း ဂျာနယ် စာတည်းအွဲ.

myan-ma naing-ngan thu. te-thăna. ăthin: dya-nè sa-di: ăpwè.

IPA transcriptions. In time the scientific principles and precise symbols of the International Phonetic Association were applied to the study and transcription of Burmese. This was advocated by Grant Brown as early as 1912, but it was first applied in detail to Burmese in 1925 by Armstrong and Pe Maung Tin. Their system was very detailed: it required the use of some fourteen special phonetic symbols and five diacritics, including some placed at various heights above the line. It was simplified by Firth (1933, 1936) to ten special symbols and two diacritics, and by Stewart (1936) to eight special symbols and two diacritics in which form it is still used (Stewart *et al.* 1940 etc., Hla Pe 1965). Further simplifications were developed in America (*e.g.* Cornyn 1944, McDavid 1945, Haas 1951, Jones and Khin 1953), reducing the special symbols to four.

In Stewart's system the example looks like this:

မြန်မာနိုင်ငံ သူတော သာ အာသင်း ဂျာနယ် စာတည်းအွဲ.

myaŋma naiŋŋaŋ θu'teθəna' ə`θiŋ janɛ sa`ti əphwɛ'

Typewritten transcriptions. The process of simplification culminated comparatively recently in a transcription which used no special symbols or diacritics and could be typed entirely on an ordinary typewriter without backspacing (Cornyn 1958, Ballard 1961). Cornyn's typewritten transcription gives:

မြန်မာနိုင်ငံ သူတောသာ အ သင်း ဂျာနယ် စာတည်းအွဲ.

myan-ma nain-ngan thu.tei-thana.qathin: ja-ne sa-di: qahpwe.

3.3 Combined systems

It would clearly be satisfactory to devise a romanization which not only showed accurately the pronunciation of a word, but also revealed its spelling in Burmese script. Some scholars have believed this impossible: "If you want to represent the speech, you must altogether neglect the spelling, and vice versa. No compromise is possible between the two", (St Barbe 1878 p.229). Duroiselle (1916 p.81) was almost as pessimistic: he thought it "would not . . . be impossible"; but it "would require a diacritical apparatus so complicated as to be more puzzling than useful".

In 1958, however, Minn Latt published just such a system, which he called "the Prague method romanization of Burmese". This was "developed slowly and gradually on research, experience and improvements" (p.156), and was "developed and experimented with gratifying results while teaching Burmese" (p.146). Minn Latt had kept to a conventional Government-type transcription for his articles on literature (1960–62), but he used his combined method when writing about grammar (1962–64). He later made some minor revisions in his romanization:

th sh š θ > *ht hs sh th*

This is the form used in his *Modernization of Burmese* (1966) and by Becková (1967).

At about the same time in America Becker was planning his own combined system, primarily for use in cataloguing Burmese books for libraries. This system was not published and is not quite complete, but the notes below include alternative suggestions taken from a typescript copy of his proposals which Becker kindly sent me in 1965.

Here is the example in the revised form of Minn Latt's romanization:

မြန်မာနိုင်ငံ သုတေသနအသင်း ဂျာနယ် စာတည်းအဖွဲ့.

myánmá náinngán thutéithăna ăthîn djáné sátîj ăphwe

3.4 Summary

For the purposes of description and discussion the various individual systems of romanization mentioned above are classified as follows:

romanization

transliteration method	transcription method				combined method
	early type	conventional type	IPA type	typewritten type	
various systems	various systems	various systems	various systems	various systems	various systems
devised, modified, or used by:					
1878 St Barbe	1800 Symes	1878 St Barbe	1925 Armstrong & PMT	1958 Cornyn	1958 Minn Latt
1913 Duroiselle	1830 Pemberton	1883 Gov't	1933 Firth	1961 Ballard	1965 Becker
1914 Blagden	1834 Crawfurd	1898 Taw Sein Ko	1936 Stewart	1965 Allott	1966 Minn Latt
1932 Luce	1845 Latter	1906 Bridges	1944 Cornyn	1968 Cornyn	1967 Bečková
1950 Hla Pe	1858 Yule	1910 Grant Brown	1945 McDavid		
1959 Than Tun	1883 Phayre	1960 Minn Latt	1951 Haas		
1960 Yi Yi	etc. (1)	1963 Butwell	1953 Jones & Khin		
1962 Ba Shin		1965 Nash	1957 Sprigg		
1963 Sprigg		1966 Lib. of Congress	1958 Minn Latt		
1965 Bernot		1967 SOAS Library	1963 Sprigg		
1965 Okell		etc. (2)	1963 Bernot		
1969 Whitbread			1965 Hla Pe		
etc.			1966 Minn Latt		
			1969 Okell		
			etc.		

(1) A few place-names survive
(2) In widespread use for names

3.4

The phrase used above to illustrate the different methods and types of romanization is set down again here for comparison. The romanizations exemplified are respectively:

transliteration method: Duroiselle's system
transcription method, early type: Latter's system
    „   „   conventional type: Grant Brown's system
    „   „   IPA type: Stewart's system
    „   „   typewritten type: Cornyn's system
combined method: Minn Latt's 1966
                                                system

မြန်မာ နိုင်ငံ သုတေသ အသင်း ဂျာနယ် စာတည်း အဖွဲ့

mranmā nuiṅṅaṁ sutesana asaṅ[3] gyǎnay cātaṅ[3] aphwai[1]
mrammā naing-gnan thŏŏtéthanǎ athěng: giānay tsadee: aphuḍy
myan-ma naing-ngan thu.te-thǎna. ǎthin: dya-nè sa-di: ǎpwè.
myaŋma naiŋŋaŋ θu'teθəna' ə`θiŋ janɛ sa`ti əphwɛ'
myan-ma naìn-ngan thu.tei-thana.qathin: ja-ne sa-di: qahpwe.
myǎnmá náinngán thutéithǎna ǎthìn djáné sátî̜ ǎphwe

4 THE THREE METHODS IN DETAIL

This section describes each of the three methods in detail by tabulating its roman equivalents and conventions. It would have been unwieldy, and would serve little purpose, to list all the symbols of all the systems within each method, so in each case one system is selected as representative of its method and set out in a table opposite the corresponding Burmese symbols or sounds. Variations from it used by other writers, and some further possibilities, are mentioned in the notes and comments which follow each table.

In commenting in the notes on the merits and faults of alternative conventions, it is assumed that the following qualities are desirable:

1. A romanization should be *unambiguous*: the same roman letter (or other symbol) should not be used for two sounds or symbols in the Burmese.

2. It should be *plausible*: conventions such as using the letter *f* to represent the sound /o/ should be avoided as far as possible.

3. It should be *easily memorized: e.g.* if the tone-marks are represented by raised figures, the figures ^{1} and ^{2} for ᥐ and ᥐ : respectively have better mnemonic value (1 = one dot, 2 = two dots) than say Duroiselle's convention of $+^1$ for "creaky" tone, $+^2$ for "level" tone, and $+^3$ for "heavy" tone.

4. It should be easily *readable: e.g.* it should avoid long strings of syllables that are not readily separated by the eye, such as:
myañmanaiññgañpyeidwìñyeijaùntheyupoúhsauñyeïåhpwé

5. It should be *traditional*: it should maintain, as far as possible, conventions that are well known and used in many other systems.

6. It should be *economical*: the fewer symbols required the better; *e.g.* to assign a separate symbol to each of three

tones is less economical than marking two of them and leaving the third recognizable by the fact that it has no mark.

7. Its symbols should be readily *available*: printers should not have to order special sorts for it, and typists should need few extra keys, or none, over and above those normally supplied.

Some kinds of writing entail quoting several lines or pages of romanized Burmese, while other kinds use only an occasional word or two here and there. This difference affects some aspects of romanization; *e.g.* writers of the latter kind often italicize or underline the romanized words, which means that italics/underlining cannot easily be used in the romanization for distinguishing individual Burmese sounds or letters. The first kind of writing is referred to here as "continuous text", and the second as "embedded words".

Writings about Burma and Burmese at the present time are mainly in English, French, Czech, German and Italian. There are also studies in Russian, Japanese and Chinese, but these languages obviously have different transcription problems. Among the roman-script languages English is given first consideration for the purposes of this booklet. This is because by far the greater part of writings on Burma today (other than those in Burmese) are in English; and because English is the chief medium of communication between Burma and the rest of the world.

Priority for English affects romanization in two ways. It affects the "plausibility" of using certain roman letters for Burmese sounds; *e.g.* the letter *j* suggests different sounds to Englishmen, Frenchmen, and Germans; and it means that the "ordinary" typewriter will not have, for example, the accents of French or Italian. In the notes below it is assumed that the standard English keyboard, in addition to the usual 26 letters, each in capital and small, figures and fractions, will have the following symbols:

* " / @ £ _ & ' ( ) + = ! - : ; ? , . %

These are taken from the Olympia English keyboard, no.7051.

4.1 Transliteration

The system set out in the Table below as representative of transliteration is that of Duroiselle 1916. Other references in which the transliteration method is used or discussed are:

1878	St Barbe	1960	Yi Yi
1913	Duroiselle	1962	Ba Shin
1914	Blagden	1963	Sprigg
1919	Duroiselle	1965	Bernot
1932	Luce	1965	Okell
1950	Hla Pe	1969	Whitbread
1959	Than Tun		

The figures in parentheses in the Table refer to the notes which follow.

4.1.1

4.1.1 Table 1: Transliteration: Duroiselle's system

Consonants

scr	က	ခ	ဂ	ဃ	င	စ	ဆ	ဇ	ဈ	ဉ	ည	ဋ	ဌ	ဍ	ဎ	ဏ	တ
Dur	k	kh	g	gh	ṅ	c	ch	j	jh	ñ	ñ	ṭ	ṭh	ḍ	ḍh	ṇ	t

(1)

scr	ထ	ဒ	ဓ	န	ပ	ဖ	ဗ	ဘ	မ	ယ	ရ	လ	ဝ	သ	ဟ	ဠ	အ
Dur	th	d	dh	n	p	ph	b	bh	m	y	r	l	w/v	s	h	ḷ	(a)

(2) (6)

Vowels

scr	+	+ာ/ါ	ိ	ီ	◌ု/ု	◌ူ/ူ	ေ+	ဲ	ေ+ာ/ို	ေ+ာ်/ော်	◌ု
	-	-	◌ိ	◌ီ	◌ု	◌ူ	◌	-	◌ော	◌ော်	-
Dur	a	ā	i	ī	u	ū	e	ai	o	o²	ui

(3) (4) (5) (6)

Finals (8)

scr	◌ံ	◌်
Dur	ṁ	space or following consonant

Medials (7)				Tone marks (9)	
scr	ျ	ြ	◌ွ	◌ှ	◌့	+:
Dur	+y	+r	+w	+h	+¹	+³

Punctuation (10)		Figures	
၊	။	၁ ၂ ၃ ၄ ၅ ၆ ၇ ၈ ၉ ၀	
၊	။ or ၌	1 2 3 4 5 6 7 8 9 0	

Abbreviations (11): in full (*e.g.* ၌ *nhuik*, ၍ *rwe¹*, etc.) but ၏ *i*

Spacing (12): syllables joined, sense-groups spaced

4.1.2 Transliteration: notes and variants

(1) ည/ဉ > ñ

Duroiselle's system was devised primarily for old texts and inscriptions where the small letter is rarely used, so he was able to use ñ for both letters of this pair without ambiguity. For modern spellings however it is important to make some provision for distinguishing the two, both initially and finally, *e.g.* in the following words:

ည် ၊ ည က် ၊   ချည် ၊ ချင့် ၊   ပ ညာ ၊ ပ ဉ္ဇ

Two methods have been used:

(*a*) Sprigg keeps ñ for the first of the pair, and uses ñ̇ for the second, which requires another diacritic

(*b*) Okell has ññ for the first and ñ for the second. This is the normal convention for transliterating Pali (*e.g. paññā* and *pañca* for the last pair in the group above) and is used for Pali words by Duroiselle himself.

(2) ဝ > w/v

Here again Duroiselle has different conventions for Burmese and Pali words: he uses *w* for Burmese but *v* for Pali; *e.g.*

ဝ က်   ဝတ္ထု   တွက်   ဒွါ ရ

wak   but   *vatthu*;   *twak*   but   *dvāra*

This is unsatisfactory, both because it is better to keep to a one-for-one correspondence between Burmese and roman, and because there are borderline cases—Pali words that are so firmly established in Burmese and altered in form that there would be inconsistencies between one writer and another; *e.g.*

Pali: ဝါ သၢ၊   ဝေဇ ယန္တ၊   ဝိ နယၢ   ဝိ ညာၢကၢ၊   ဝဉ္

> Burmese: ဝါ ၊   ဝေ ယန်၊   ဝိ နည်း၊   ဝိ ညာၢၣ်   ဝၣ်

It is preferable therefore to discard *v* and use *w* throughout.

(3) ႞ > *ai*

Bernot has *è* (p.462), presumably on the grounds that it is a more plausible representation of the pronunciation. This however is a small gain and does not outweigh the losses, which are that it requires yet another diacritic, departs from the conventions of other writers, and loses the connection with established usage for Sanskrit.

(4) ၎ +ာ > o^2

Duroiselle's convention treats these symbols as the vowel *o* with a tone-mark (/shei.htou:/), which is not very satisfactory: see (9) below. Variants are as follows:

(*a*) Blagden suggests *au*, on the basis of the similarity in alphabetical ordering with Sanskrit.

(*b*) Luce, Yi Yi, Than Tun, and Ba Shin have *oau*, which enables them to use *au* for the Old Burmese abbreviation written with /shei.htou:/ alone; *e.g.*

ဪ for ၎ောၡ   ၬ for ၎ောၥ

(*c*) Hla Pe and Whitbread use *ô*, an extra diacritic.

(*d*) Okell treats this vowel and the one which precedes it in the alphabet as a pair corresponding to *a ā, i ī, u ū*, and so writes *o ō*. This does not preclude the use of *au* for the Old Burmese convention in (*b*) above, and requires no new diacritic.

(5) ၌ > *ui*

This vowel is not used in Pali or Sanskrit so a new convention has had to be devised for it. Duroiselle's *ui* has been criticized on the grounds that it is far removed from the pronunciation, and that if the two symbols which make up this vowel are to be transliterated separately (*u* and *i*), then the two that make up *o* should be treated in the same way as *eā*.

The retention of *ui* is favoured however by a number of considerations. Since *o* is already in use for another vowel, there is no plausible alternative (? *ou*, or *oe*) that does not introduce more diacritics. *Ui* has been in use over the past century (since St Barbe, 1878) for both Burmese and Mon, and it corresponds well with vowels in related languages which are transcribed *ü, üi, oi*, etc. (Duroiselle 1916 p.84). It is also useful for transliterating Old Burmese where this vowel is often written *uw* or *iw* in open syllables and *i* in closed syllables.

(6) ရူ ဤ ၉ ၆ ၄ ၏ ၎

These symbols are referred to here as "special vowel symbols", as against the spelling of the same syllables which uses the "vowel support" အ , i.e.

အိ အီ အု အူ ေအ ေအာ ေအာ်

Some words, especially in older texts, may be spelt either with the special vowel symbols or with the vowel support, and it may be useful for some purposes to know which method is used, but Duroiselle's system does not distinguish between them.

Whitbread symbolizes the vowel support in some vowels by *a,* and its absence then shows that a special vowel symbol is used; *e.g.*

ဤ   အီ   ၉တ်   အုတ်   (but ၏   ေအာ်

ī   *aī*   *ut*   *aut*   *ō*   *ô*)

This is not easy to read, especially in words with the prefix *a-*; *e.g.*

အဲ   အအိမ်

a-ai   *a-aim*

Various other devices are possible: a full stop could be placed after the vowel to show it is spelt with a special symbol (perhaps awkward to read); the special vowel symbols could be transliterated by capital letters (awkward for names); or they could be underlined/italicized (awkward for embedded words which are underlined/italicized anyway).

A more satisfactory convention is used by Sprigg 1965: the presence of the vowel support is shown by a raised comma (printed ' typed') before the vowel. Its absence indicates a special vowel symbol: *e.g.* he would transliterate the above words *i 'i ut 'ut.* This convention is easy to type and print, and is ambiguous in typing only with the single quotation mark—an ambiguity which is not likely to occur frequently. If necessary, the ambiguity can be removed by extending the underlining to the raised comma in typewriting, or, if underlining is not being used, by enclosing Burmese words between oblique strokes (or some other convenient symbol); *e.g.* ". . . the word /'a'im/ has a rather different meaning . . ."

4.1.2

(7) ဗ ြြ ဋ ဌ

As the medial consonants in Burmese script do not succeed one another on the line, the order in which their romanized equivalents are placed is arbitrary. It is customary to write them in an order which bears some relation to the way they are pronounced: *h, y* or *r, w; e.g.*

မှ ြြုပ် လွာ ကျွန် ကြွက် မြွာ
mhya   mhrup   lhwā   kywan   krwak   mhrwā

(8) ့

Duroiselle's system does not mark this symbol (/ätha¹/), with the result that when transliterated syllables are run together there is no means of knowing whether a consonant is final or initial, or if it is conjunct; *e.g.*

his *sakhaṅ*	could be	သ၈င်	or	သက် ဟင်
„ *limmo²*	„ „	လိ မ္မော်	„	လိ မ် မော်
„ *atuikok*	„ „	အ တို ကောက်	„	အက်အိုက်အောက်etc.
„ *aphracapyak*	„ „	အ ြြစ် အ ပျက်	„	အ ြြ စ ပ် ယက် etc.

There are several ways of overcoming, or at least easing, this difficulty.

(*a*) Each syllable can be separated from the next by a space—a method which Duroiselle makes use of to some extent. This removes all ambiguities but is not easy to read; *e.g.*

ဝ ကား ဝ မ ည် ြြောြြီး အ မ ရ ပူ ရ ြြန် ြြ သ ည်
ca kā³ ca mañ pro pri³ a ma ra pū ra pran kra sañ

(*b*) Marking the vowel support by a raised comma—see (6) above—removes most initial/final ambiguities (*e.g.* ¹*atuikok*), but does not help with initial/medial ambiguities (*e.g.* ¹*aphrac*)

(*c*) Ba Shin often—but not always—marks combined consonants (*i.e.* conjunct, or initial with medial) by = or ◡ ; *e.g.*

နှိက္ကာ ထွတ္တဒွန် အ မ တျာ သ ကြာ
nhik=kā   thwaṭṭadwan   amatyā   sakrā

This is a help, but again is not a complete solution; *e.g.* it does not clarify *atuikok*; and ◡ is an awkward diacritic.

22

(*d*) Perhaps the most logical answer is to have some mark corresponding to the /ätha¹/. One might use, for example, the raised comma, which is positioned rather like the /ätha¹/ in the Burmese script. This would give

လက်မှတ် နှစ်စောင် ဝယ်လိုက်သည်

lak¹mhat¹ nhac¹coṅ¹ way¹luik¹san¹

The raised comma used in this way would remove the final/initial and initial/medial ambiguities; it is easy to read and print or type, and it helps to separate syllables. There are however two disadvantages: first the relatively minor one that it would preclude the use of the raised comma for the special vowel/vowel support problem of note (6); and the more serious one that it is uneconomical. Any consonant followed by a space, by a tone-mark, or by a vowel support symbol (if one were adopted) cannot be other than final, and it would be redundant to have an extra mark to show that it is final.

(*e*) Since the cases in which a final consonant needs to be specially marked as such are limited, one could compromise by· using some symbol (e.g. a hyphen) only when necessary, i.e. when the consonant is not already shown to be final by a space, tone-mark, or vowel support symbol. The hyphen would therefore be required between a final and an initial consonant, and between a final and a special vowel symbol. Its absence would also be significant; *e.g.*

lak-phak-rañ	<	လက်ဖက်ရည်	not	လက်ဖျြည်
jarak-u	„	ဇရက်ဥ	„	ဇရကု
cakkū	„	စက္ကူ	„	စက်ကူ
taṇhā	„	တဏှာ	„	တန်ဟာ
maṅgalā	„	မင်္ဂလာ	„	မင်္ဂလာ

For Duroiselle's *ṁ* Whitbread writes *m* when there is no subscript tone-mark, but *ṁ* when there is: *ṃ̇*.

(9) ţ > +⁴   +: > +³

Duroiselle's convention of raised numbers accords with practice in the romanization of some other tone languages, but it is

23

not very suitable for transliterating Burmese since the marks of tone in the script do not correspond regularly with the tones in the speech. All syllables ending with a vowel or final nasal, for example, can be pronounced in Duroiselle's "second" tone, yet his raised *2* is needed only for the vowel *o* and for no others. The distribution of his raised *1* and *3* is not quite so restricted, but there are several syllables pronounced in the first and third tones which have no mark in the script to show it and so cannot have *1* and *3* in their transliteration. It would be preferable therefore to use a convention which paid less attention to the pronunciation and more to the script.

In fact the "length mark" ⊤ on *ā, ī, ū* accounts for three of what are effectively tone-marks in the script; and if it is used for *ō* as well, as suggested in note (4), the only remaining tone-marks which need a roman equivalent are ⨎ and ⊹: Possibilities for these two are:

(*a*) ⨎¹ ⨎²   awkward for typing

(*b*) ⊹. ⊹:   Bernot; possible ambiguity with full stop and colon in embedded words unless covered by oblique strokes or underlining

(*c*) ⨎̣ ⊹:   ⊹. above is preferable to ⨎̣ as the latter does not help to separate syllables (see (12) below) and in typewriting makes difficulties for underlining

(*d*) ⨎̧ ⊹:   Whitbread; uses an extra diacritic, other difficulties as for (*c*)

(*e*) ⊹, ⊹:   Yi Yi; as for (*b*), and ⊹, is less like the dot of the script

(*f*) ⊹' ⊹:   Sprigg 1965 (in typewritten text); ⊹' not available if used for the vowel support: see (6)

(*g*) ⊹' ⊹⸴   Sprigg 1963: ⊹' ambiguous with quotation mark, ⊹⸴ not easy to type and print

(*h*) ⊹' ⊹ḥ   Ba Shin; *ḥ* is used for the same symbol in Sanskrit, but is perhaps not very plausible for Burmese (*e.g. taññh, maṅh-sāh*)

(*i*) ⊹' ⊹"   Okell; awkward to type, unless one uses ' and " which are ambiguous with quotation marks

(*j*) ⨎́ ⨎̀   does not help to separate syllables

(10) *Punctuation marks*

Duroiselle's conventions here make difficulties for typing and printing. It is not easy to choose equivalents from among the roman punctuation marks (, ; : .) since Burmese texts use ॥ sometimes where roman would use a comma or colon, and sometimes where roman would use a full stop. Perhaps better equivalents here would be oblique strokes: / and //. These may be already in use for marking off embedded words (see note (6) above), but it is rarely necessary to mark punctuation with embedded words: it is normally shown only in continuous texts where marking off is not needed.

(11) *Abbreviations*

Duroiselle writes out abbreviations in full, except for ၍ for which he writes *i*, the same as his equivalent for ၌ and ၏ ॥ Okell uses *í* for the abbreviated syllable to avoid this ambiguity.

Abbreviations are not often likely to be of great importance, but it may sometimes be of interest to know whether a text uses abbreviated forms or not. Various devices suggest themselves:

(*a*) Some abbreviations could be written out as they stand; *e.g.*

ရင်း   ၎င်   နှက်   သွောက်
4ń[3]   *eń*[1]   *naṁk*   *swok*

but this is not possible for all, particularly the common three:

၏   ၍   ၌

(*b*) One could write out an abbreviated syllable in full but show that it is abbreviated by placing a full stop after it. This however would preclude the use of the full stop as a tone-mark.

(*c*) Abbreviation could be shown by using an accent; *e.g.*

၍   ၌   ကြောင်
rwé[1]   *nhúik*   *króń*[1]

but this introduces yet another diacritic.

(*d*) One could underline/italicize abbreviated syllables, but this would be awkward for embedded words which are already underlined/italicized.

(*e*) Perhaps the least unsatisfactory answer would be to star abbreviated syllables. This need be done only if it is desired to show abbreviations; *e.g.*

ခုံ ပေါ် ၌   ထွင်း ၍   နေ သော ၏

khuṁpo²*nhuik   thuiṅ*rwe¹   neso*kroṅ¹

For this purpose the full form of ၏ may be taken either as အံ a form used in Pagan period inscriptions, or as အည် which is used in verse for rhyme and occasionally in old prose texts. If the vowel support is romanized ', these two spellings would be transliterated *e'* and *eñ¹* respectively.

(12) *Spacing*

Duroiselle's practice of separating "words" or sense-groups from each other by space, and running together the syllables within a group, is much more easily readable than texts in which each syllable is separated from the next by space. Within the groups the separation of syllables from each other is helped by tone-marks, and would be further helped by the adoption of the raised comma for the vowel support, and the hyphen for finals where necessary. There would still be cases however which are confusing to the eye: long groups of syllables not parted by spaces, tone-marks, raised commas or hyphens; *e.g.*

ရှာဖွေ လို့ လာ ကြပါ သ တ ည်း

rhāphweluilākrapāsatañ³

Consecutive vowels also look unsightly:

ေတာ ် င ေတာ င်   ဣ ဤ   ဧ ဧ   ဥ ဩ

toṅ-toṅ   *ii*   *ee*   *uo*

For such cases hyphens could be used as seems appropriate to aid the eye. This would not give rise to ambiguity with the use of the hyphen to mark final consonants; *e.g.*

rhāphwe-luilā-krapā-satañ³   *toṅ-toṅ i-i*   *e-e*   *u-o*

(13) *Sanskrit letters*

Burmese transliterations of Sanskrit words—or at least letters—are occasionally found in learned texts. This entails the use of symbols additional to the regular alphabet shown above, but the available sources do not agree on the forms of all the symbols.

Those shown below are taken from:

S သာ၌ု ြြ္ဟာ   (c.1750) by တောင် တွင်း ဆရာတော်၊ ရာမညတိုင်း၊ ရန်ကုန်၊ ၄ နှစ် ၁၀၇၂။p.3

V ဓေဟာဒ ရက္ခ ပကာ သာနီ   (c.1800) by ၃ တိယ ကျော်အောင်စံထား ဆရာတော်၊တို့၊ ရန်ကုန် ၁၉၃၆။ p.106

A အမရ ကာ ၈   (c.1930) by ဘာ ဘ ယ ရာ မ ဆရာတော် (ရေးကူ) ဂူကာ လက်ရ ရန်ကုန်၊ ၁၉၃၀။ p.၅

It looks as if the first two authorities give traditional forms while the translator of the last has in some cases invented new ones. All three works give approximations to the pronunciation in Burmese script, which are also listed below (pron.). The roman equivalents shown as rom. are from the transliteration tables at the end of each volume of the Journal of the Royal Asiatic Society from 1912 to 1928. Monier-Williams' *Sanskrit English Dictionary* (rev. ed. Oxford University Press 1899) has different equivalents, so his are shown as well (MW), though the JRAS equivalents now have wider currency.

S	၃	၃	၉	၉	၈	၀	၈	၈	–	–
V	„	၃	၈	၈	„	„	„	„	–	–
A	၈	၈	၉	၈	„	„	–	–	၈	၀

	+ၫ	+ၫ	၉	၈						
pron.	ရ်/ရို့	ရီ/ရို	လိ/လို့	လီ/လို	ယ္	၈/၈ရ	က	၀	၈/၉	၈/၉
						သ/ရ	(လွှာဂ၈)(နူတ်ဝမ်)			

| rom. | r̥ | r̥̄ | l̥ | l̥/l̥ | ś | s | h | h | r | rh |
| MW | ri | rī | lri | lrī | ś | sh | – | – | – | – |

4.1.3 Summary

Duroiselle's system contains a few points which cause awkwardness or ambiguities. Of the possible amendments and alternatives discussed in the notes above those which seem most satisfactory are:

4.1.3

note (1) *ñ*   also use *ññ*
    (2) *v*   omit, using *w* throughout
    (4) o^2 use *ō*
    (6) *special vowels*   show by omission of raised comma
    (8) *tone-marks*   use +. and +:
    (9) *finals*   use hyphen where required
    (10) *punctuation*   use / and //
    (11) *abbreviations*   use *+ if desired
    (12) *spacing*   use hyphen at discretion

A transliteration system incorporating these amendments is recommended for certain purposes in Section 5. It is set out in full in Table 4 (Section 7.1), and is referred to as "standard transliteration" to distinguish it from "simplified transliteration" which is discussed below.

The "standard transliteration" suggested above uses no more diacritics than the widely used transliteration system for Pali: ᵻ ᵼ ᵼ ᵼ. These however are extravagantly used: ᵼ is needed for only one letter (*ñ*); ᵻ for only two (*ṅ ṁ*); and ᵼ and ᵼ for only three letters each (*t d n, ā ī ū*). But for the need to have four different kinds of *n* (*n ṅ ñ n*) it would have been possible to use only one diacritic for the whole system. While it is impossible to amend these four diacritics in such a way as to make the system convenient for typing on an ordinary typewriter without making transliterated Pali words hard to recognize, it is not difficult to halve their number. One could dispense with ᵼ and ᵻ by altering *ṅ* to *ng*
            ṁ to *m*
            ñ to *ṅ*

This gives a simplified transliteration very little loss of clarity; *e.g.*

မောင်ပုည တနေ့လုံး လေးဖြိုး စဉ်းစားနေသောလည်း အကြံ မရ

standard:
     moṅ puñña tane.luṁ: ṅe:pri: cañ:cā:nesōlaññ: ˡakraṁ mara
simplified:
     mong puñña tane. lum: nge:pri: cañ:cā:nesōlaññ: ˡakram mara

The remaining two diacritics (᷁ and ᵼ) can either be put on a typewriter, or, if this is not convenient, they must be added to the page by hand. For those who have much to do with Burmese an advantage of having these two diacritics on the typewriter is that they are also used for the standard conventional transcription set out in Table 5 (Section 7.1.2).

The short passage of classical verse given below illustrates the use of the standard transliteration and its simplified variation.

script	transliteration: standard	simplified
ထို က ဆက် ညီ	thui-ka chak-ññī	thui-ka chak-ññī ·
မင်း ၄၃ဝိ တို့	man: ṭhāwī-tui.	mang:thāwī-tui.
ဝဇိ ရ ပြ ညီ	Wajīra-prañ̃	Wajīra-prañ̃
ဆ က် ရ ညီ ဆုံး ဿ	chak-rhañ̃ chum:tha	chak-rhañ̃ chum:tha
ဿာ ဓိ န မှ	Sādhina-mha	Sādhina-mha
ခင် လှ မျိုး နွယ်	khañ-lha myui:nway	khang-lha myui:nway
နှစ် ဆ ယ့် နှင့် ရှစ်	nhac-chay-nhañ. rhac	nhac-chay-nhang. rhac
တ ညီ လ စ် မြို့ ပြ	tañ̃-lac mrui. pra	tañ̃-lac mrui. pra
မ ဓု ရ ဝယ်	Madhura-way	Madhura-way
ဓ မ္မ ဂု တ် လျှင်	Dhammagut-lhyañ	Dhammagut-lhyang
အ ဆုံး ရှင် *ဧ	ˈachuṁ: rhwañ-*eˡ	ˈachum: rhwang-*eˡ

from: ငဝဉ် ကျ မင်း နားတော်သွင်း ချင်း by ပလိပ်ရှာစား ဦးဖျော်၊ တံသာဝတီ၊ ရန်ကုန် ၊ ၃ နိပ ၁၉၆၁ p.21 (v.9)

4.2 Transcription

Of the four types of transcription set out below, the first, representing the early type, is taken from Latter, and the last, representing the typewritten type, from Cornyn 1958. The remaining two types, conventional and IPA, are not represented by the conventions of any single system, but are made up in order to highlight the characteristics of the type and bring out its differences from the others. The system shown as conventional is close to Grant Brown, and that shown as IPA is close to Sprigg 1963.

The following are writers who have devised, modified or used transcription systems.

4.2

Early type	Conventional type	IPA type	Typewritten type
1800 Symes	1878 St Barbe	1925 Armstrong	1958 Cornyn
1830 Pemberton	1883 Government	& Pe Maung Tin	1961 Ballard
1834 Crawfurd	1898 Taw Sein Ko	1933 Firth	1965 Allott
1845 Latter	1906 Bridges	1936 Stewart	1966 Bernot
1853 Phayre	1910 Grant Brown	1944 Cornyn	
1858 Yule	1960 Minn Latt	1945 McDavid	
	1963 Butwell	1951 Haas	
	1965 Nash	1953 Jones	
	1966 Lib.Cong.	& Khin	
	1967 Lib.SOAS	1957 Sprigg	
	n.d. St John	1958 Minn Latt	
		1963 Bernot	
		1963 Sprigg	
		1965 Hla Pe	
		1966 Minn Latt	
		1969 Okell	

4.2.1 Table 2: Transcription: early, conventional, IPA and typewritten types

Initials:

Plosives etc.: aspirate (1)

						plain					voiced (3)					
Early	{ *,kh ht hp khi tsh*					*khy*	*k t p ki*	*ts th*			*z s*	*g d b*	*gy dz* –			*gh dh bh*
Conv	*k̆ t̆ p̆ ch*	*s̆*					*k t p ky*	*s th*				*g d b*	*gy z*	th		
IPA	*kh th ph tɕh*	*sh*					*k t p tɕ*	*s θ*				*g d b*	*dʑ z*	*ð*		
Typed	*hk ht hp hc*	*hs*					*k t p c*	*s th*				*g d b*	*j*	*z*	*dh*	
	(2)						(2)					(2)			(4)	

Nasals etc.(6): aspirate							plain						Others		
Early	{ *gnh hn hm hgny*			*hl sh hw*			*gn n m gny*		*l y w*				*r h* –		
							ll								
Conv	*hng hn hm hny*			*hl sh hw*			*ng n m ny*		*l y w*				*r h* –		
IPA	*ŋ̊ n̥ m̥ ɲ̊*			*l̥ ɕ w̥*			*ŋ n m ɲ*		*l j w*				*ɾh ʔ*		
Typed	*hng hn hm hny*			*hl sh hw*			*ng n m ny*		*l y w*				*r h q*		
	(5)												(7)		

Vowels (8): open syllables									closed syllables						
Early	{ *ee é ey a au ō*					*oo ă*			*ee ie ai ā ou ŏŏ ŏ ĕ/ie*						
	ie ay								*ĕ/e ŏi*						
Conv	*i e è a aw o*					*u ă*			*i ei ai a au o u e*						
IPA	*i e ɛ a ɔ o*					*u ə*			*ɿ eɿ aɿ a aɵ oɵ ɵ ɛ*						
Typed	*i ei e a o*					*ou u a*			*i ei ai a au ou u e*						

Medials:			Finals (9):		Tones (10):			Voicing (11):
Early	*y/i*	*w/u/o*	+*t/k* +*n/ng*		+ + +:			write in
Conv	*y*	*w*	+*t/k* +*n/ng*		+ + ꞋＩ			write in
IPA	*j*	*w*	+ʔ ꞋＩ		_+ ꞋＩ ꞋＩ			spacing
Typed	*y*	*w*	+ꞌ +*n.*		+ +. +:			write in

Spacing (12):

Early	syllables joined, sense-groups spaced
Conv	syllables joined, sense-groups spaced
IPA	space at "open juncture"
Typed	syllables separated by tone-marks, sense-groups spaced

4.2.2

4.2.2 Transcription: notes and variants

(1) *Aspirate plosives, etc.*

Except for *ky* and *ch* (=/c, hc/), the Government *Tables* do not distinguish aspirate from plain, but "the aspirated letter may be distinguished if so desired from the unaspirated by the use of an apostrophe, thus . . . 'k" (1890 p.ii). This symbolization is used by Taw Sein Ko; Grant Brown has *k̇*, etc.

Perhaps the neatest way of showing aspiration in plosives is to write an *h* after the plain consonant, as in IPA; but this is liable to be mispronounced by the uninitiated Englishman (*th*, *ph*, *sh*) and also makes it necessary to devise other symbols (*e.g.* IPA's *θ, ɕ*) for the dental and palato-alveolar fricatives. Hence the preceding *h* of the typewritten type, which leaves *th* and *sh* free for the fricatives. Minn Latt uses an acute accent (*ḱ t́ ṕ ć ś*) which neatly matches the aspirate nasals (*ń m̀* etc.). The disadvantages of a preceding *h* are that it is misleading for pronunciation, and it makes a disproportionately heavy load on *h* in abbreviations using initials.

(2) *Palatal affricates*

Some writers prefer *ty* to *ky* for /c/ on the grounds that it helps foreigners to the correct pronunciation (*e.g.* Jones and Khin, Ballard, Grant Brown); hence also *dy* for /j/ (Jones and Khin, Grant Brown), and *thy* for /hc/ (Jones and Khin). In fact it is arguable whether *ty*, which suggests a palatalized alveolar, is more likely to bring a non-Burmese speaker to this unfamiliar sound than *ky*, which suggests a palatalized velar. *Ky* reflects Burmese spelling; *c* is perhaps the neatest convention, corresponding well with the *ch* (/hc/) used by some IPA-type systems, but is mispronounced by the uninitiated. Some Indian names are transcribed with *ch* and *chh* for plain and aspirate, a convention that does not seem to have been used for Burmese. Another possibility is to use *ci gi* as in Italian *ciao, Giorgio*, but this would be awkward before *i, e.g. cii:* for /ci:/.

(3) *Voiced consonants*

Sprigg's narrow transcription shows fricative pronunciations of /g d b/ as *ɣ r β*.

(4) *Voiced dental fricative*

Both English spelling and Burmese script lack a distinctive symbolization of this sound: they use the same letters as for the unvoiced fricative. Some conventional transcriptions do likewise, using *th* for both (Grant Brown, Government); others distinguish the voiced sound by italics/underlining or by roman type if the rest of the transcription is italicized (Bridges, Taw Sein Ko, Ballard). Some writers (*e.g.* McDavid) treat the voicing of /th/ as a juncture-feature only which eliminates the need for an extra symbol since the juncture marking (*e.g.* absence of space between syllables) sufficiently indicates the voiced pronunciation. This method however cannot represent the literary-style word /dhou./, occasionally heard in colloquial speech, which is often sentence-initial, as in

သို့ သော် လည်း   /dhou. dho-le:/

သို့ တ လည်း မဟုတ်   /dhou. di: mähou¹/

Apart from IPA's *ð* and typewritten *dh*, only one other symbolization seems to have been devised: Minn Latt 1966 has *đ*. Bernot 1966, rather implausibly, uses *ç* for both the voiced and the unvoiced phonemes.

(5) *Hush sibilant*

Also rendered *š* (Cornyn 1944, Bernot, Minn Latt), *ʂ* (Armstrong and Pe Maung Tin, Sprigg). *Sh* is an obvious choice for English speakers unless one is using a following *h* for aspirate plosives, etc. Minn Latt's 1958 combined system actually used *hs* for the sibilant /sh/ in order to keep *sh* for the aspirate /hs/. Another possibility, *hy*, is supported by such verb pairs as

လျော့   /yo./   "be slack"   ရှော့   /sho./   "make slack"

ရွေ့   /ywei./   "be moved"   ရွှေ့   /shwei./   "cause to move"

It is neat to be able to transcribe these as /yo. hyo./, /ywei. hywei./. This convention is used by Cornyn 1968 and Okell.

(6) *Nasal consonants*

Several systems of the IPA type achieve neatness and avoid some ambiguities by keeping to a single letter (such as those in the table) for each of the four nasal initials. Minn Latt 1966 and Bernot 1963 achieve the same result by using diacritics, so avoiding the need for special letters: Minn Latt has ṅ n m ň, and Bernot 1963 has ñ n m ñ. St John, reprinted as recently as the early 1960s, preserves *gn* as in the early transcriptions.

(7) *Glottal onset*

Not indispensable, since it is not phonemically distinctive, and indeed not always present: one hears both *sa-qou*[i] and *sa-ou*[l]. Its main advantage is in dividing syllables (*e.g. taqoqo* is more easily readable than *taoo*), and, in Cornyn's 1958 system, in distinguishing the short central vowel before another vowel (*e.g. taqin-ga* as against *tain-ga* = ကအနီ၊ တ္တိင်္ ဂ).

(8) *Vowels*

The fundamental problem here is that the roman alphabet offers only five plausible vowel letters to represent 15 Burmese vowels and diphthongs. The size of the problem can be much reduced by merging the vowels of the open syllables with the vowels and diphthongs of the closed syllables, *i.e.* using the same symbolization for similar sounds in each category. This overlooks the difference shown in some IPA-type systems between the *i a u* of open syllables and the *ɪ a o* of closed syllables, and between IPA's (open) *e o* and (closed) *ei ou*. Most systems merge to some extent, though few go so far as to merge all eight vowels in each category. The eighth open and the eighth closed in the Table above cannot plausibly be merged, and no system merges both the third open and closed and the fifth open and closed (/e/ with /ai/, /o/ with /au/), though St Barbe suggests *ai* for both the third vowels, and Bernot 1963 uses *ɔ* for both the fifth vowels. The plausibility of these mergers could be supported by *ai* in French *vrai* and English *aisle, au* in English *haul* and German *haus*.

The most problematical, and so the most varied, vowels are the second and third open, and the sixth and fifth open. They have been transcribed variously as follows:

Stewart	e	ɛ	o	ɔ
Grant Brown	e	è	o	aw
Bernot 1966	é	è	ô	o
Cornyn	ei	e	ou	o
McDavid	ey	e	ow	o
Ballard	ey	eh	o	aw
St Barbe	ê	è	o	oa
Latter	é	ey/ay	ō	au

Almost as difficult is the weak vowel (eighth open), which is rendered ə in strict IPA-type systems, ă by Grant Brown, Minn Latt 1966 and Okell, a (without tone-mark) in simplified IPA and typewritten systems, except Bernot 1966 who has e. There are reasons for using a diacritic for this sound: see the summary (4.2.3) below. A similar sound is written v in Rawang (*e.g. Rvwang*) but this seems unacceptably implausible.

Before leaving the vowel problem it is worth noting what a large number of alternative possibilities there is to choose from, when one takes the five "vowel" letters of the roman alphabet singly, in pairs, and before *y, w* or *h*.

i	*ii*	*ie*	*ia*	*io*	*iu*	*iy*	*iw*	*ih*
e	*ei*	*ee*	*ea*	*eo*	*eu*	*ey*	*ew*	*eh*
a	*ai*	*ae*	*aa*	*ao*	*au*	*ay*	*aw*	*ah*
o	*oi*	*oe*	*oa*	*oo*	*ou*	*oy*	*ow*	*oh*
u	*ui*	*ue*	*ua*	*uo*	*uu*	*uy*	*uw*	*uh*

This table alone offers 45 possibilities, and the number can be greatly increased by the use of accents and other diacritics (*e.g.* ạ ậ ẩ ẫ ẩ ậ ậ), though of course not all of them make very plausible renderings of the Burmese vowel phonemes (*e.g. iu, oa*). There are however enough to allow separate renderings for the vowels of open and closed syllables, and to reflect in the transcription the symmetry of the Burmese vowel system.

The first, fourth and seventh vowels in open and closed syllables, for example, could be distinguished in some such way as this:

closed	*i*	*a*	*u*
open	*ii*	*aa*	*uu*
or	*ee*	*aa*	*oo*
or	*ih*	*ah*	*uh*
or	*iy*	*ah*	*uw*
or	*ie*	*ae*	*ue*

35

4.2.2

The second and third, and sixth and fifth vowels could be represented as:

closed *ei ai ou au* as Eng. *vein, aisle, mould,* Germ. *Kraut*
open *ey ay ow aw* as Eng. *hey, ay,   crow,   caw*

Some of the more unlikely English spellings could be used as mnemonic support for other renderings; *e.g. ea oa*

as in *great boat* for the second and sixth open or closed
or as in *bread soar* for the third and fifth open.

Analogies suggest yet other possibilities; *e.g.* if the second and third vowels open are rendered (after French spellings as in Bernot 1966) *é è,* then the sixth and fifth could be written analogously as *ó ò.* Even without using implausible renderings, then, the range of alternatives is very wide.

(9) *Finals*

Most conventional systems distribute their alternatives *t/k* and *n/ng* among different vowels as follows:

it eik aik at auk ok ut et
in ein aing an aung on un −

This distribution seems to have been arrived at partly under the influence of Burmese spelling (*aik aing, auk aung*) and partly by what foreigners believed they were hearing when confronted with the unfamiliar glottal stop and nasalization.

Final nasal is written *ŋ* by Stewart, Firth and Minn Latt 1958, *ṅ* by Minn Latt 1966 and Bernot 1963. It is curious that no one seems to have used *q* for final glottal stop.

In some IPA-type transcriptions (*e.g.* Sprigg, Cornyn 1944) and in Bernot 1966, assimilation of finals is shown; *e.g.*

*sitta*¹ for /si¹ta¹/
wim-ba for /win-ba/ etc.

Armstrong and Pe Maung Tin show assimilation of nasal final but not of stop final.

(10) *Tones*

Some of the earlier conventional systems use a form of transliteration for the vowels and tones; *e.g.* Bridges has

a i u e è aw o
ā ī ū e è āw o ă
ā: ī: ū: e: è: aw o:

36

Taw Sein Ko has a similar convention, and St John, whose curious transcription is described as "in accord with Marlborough's popular phonetic system", has

ă̆ẖ	ĕĕ	ŏŏ	ạy	eh	aw̥	ŏẖ	
āẖ	ee	oo	ay	eh	āw	oẖ	ăẖ
āẖ:	ee:	oo:	ay:	eh	aw	ôẖ:	

Small circles, as used for certain syllables in the Burmese script itself (┼ ┼:), are used by Ballard, Grant Brown and St John. They are. clear, but difficult to type and print. Cornyn 1958 simplified these to dots, *i.e.* the full stop and colon (┼. ┼:), which avoids the typing/printing difficulty but can raise ambiguities with English punctuation for embedded words unless the romanization is enclosed in boundary marks such as / . . . /. Cornyn's hyphen for the level tone is omitted when the syllable is followed by space.

Accents are used in various ways by different writers; *e.g.*

မန်	မန့်	မန်း	
⊥┼	┼′	┾	Armstrong and Pe Maung Tin
┼	┼′	⸜┼	Firth 1934
⊥┼	┼	⸜┼	Firth 1933
┼	┼′	⸜┼	Stewart
⊥┼	⸝┼	⸜┼	Sprigg 1963
┼	┼	┼	Okell
┼	┼	┼	Bernot
┼	┼	┼	Cornyn 1944, McDavid, Minn Latt 1958
┼	┼	┼	Minn Latt 1966

The advantage of accents is that they are clear and unobtrusive, but they are not always available on typewriters. Bernot's accents are ambiguous: her *ci´jiṅ* could be either /ci.jin/ or /ci-jin:/. Armstrong and Pe Maung Tin use a much more detailed set of symbols than the bare three shown above: they have a pitch mark for syllables with stop final and show relative pitch for all tones. Sprigg 1957 does not as a rule mark syllable tone, but he indicates length by **+:** and occasionally writes **+'** for **/+./**.

Unwanted letters from the typewriter keyboard are used for marking tone by Jones and Khin and by Haas:

+ν +q +x for
/+   +.   +:/

This method has an attractive simplicity, but is by no means easy to read; *e.g.*

ကိုက်စား၍ အကြံ ဖြစ်ပေါ်လာတယ်
kaiᵗsaxbouq ᵗatᵧanv phyiᵗ povlavdev

Choice of tone-marks is also affected by considerations of syllable-division: see the summary below (4.2.3).

Newcomers to Burmese are sometimes apt to feel that tones are unimportant and need not be marked in a romanization. This is a mistake. Without tones Burmese would have only three possible endings to a syllable: open, nasal, and stop (/**+** **+n** **+'**/). Tones increase this number to seven: three open syllables, three with nasal final, and one with stop final (/**+** **+.** **+:**, **+n** **+n.** **+n:**, **+'** /). They are therefore as important to Burmese as final consonants are to English: they differentiate Burmese syllables in much the same way as their final consonants differentiate the English syllables *pick, pit, pip*. It is true that speakers of Burmese can sometimes recognise combinations of Burmese syllables written without tones—just as a speaker of English might guess what was meant by *don't pi' the flowers*; but one or two syllables without an identifying context are mystifying: does *su* mean /su/ "protrude", /su./ "collect", or /su:/ "pierce"? Burmese transcribed without tone-marks then, is incomplete and often ambiguous.

(11) *Voicing*

Voicing is the phenomenon seen in the alternative pronunciations of, for example, the word for "writing": in some contexts /sa/, in others /za/; *e.g.*

| အင်္ဂလိပ်စာ | /in:gälei'sa/ | "English writing" |
| ဗမာစာ | /bäma-za/ | "Burmese writing" |

This happens with 6 plain consonants: / k t p c s th/
and 5 aspirate consonants: /hk ht hp hc hs — /
whose voiced equivalents are: / g d b j z dh/
Most systems simply write (as in the above example) the
voiced consonant instead of the plain or aspirate one. In
language teaching however it is a convenience if a word has the
same form wherever it is met: *i.e.* not to find it as /sa/ in one
place and /za/ in another, but to keep to the unvoiced form /sa/
throughout. In this case it becomes necessary to use some device
to show that voicing occurs.

Some systems use a diacritic: Stewart, in his early sections,
places a small *v* over or under consonants pronounced with
voicing; and Okell uses underlining for the same purpose: *e.g.*

Stewart: *bəmaṣa*   Okell: *bămaṣa*

Other systems use space (Minn Latt 1966, the remainder of
Stewart): if voicing occurs in the initial of a syllable, the
syllable is joined to the preceding syllable (with the sign + in
Minn Latt); if voicing does not occur, the syllables are separated
by space; *e.g.*

Stewart's `yethha` is pronounced /yei:da:/
but his `ye thha` is pronounced /yei:tha:/
There are difficulties with both methods.

The use of spacing for voicing entails some sacrifice of spacing
by sense-groups, which diminishes readability; *e.g.* the two syllables of loan-words like /lo:ka./ and /kaun-si/ have to be written
apart as if they were each two separate monosyllabic "words":
/lo: ka./, /kaun si/. When this conflict occurs, Stewart in fact
sacrifices voicing to sense; *e.g.* his *bəhu'θu'ta'* is /bähu.thu.ta./
not, as the spacing suggests, /bähu.dhu.da./. The diacritics that
have been used to mark voicing also have their snags: Stewart's
v is awkward to type and print, while Okell's underlining requires
special sorts for printing and presents problems for typing when
embedded words are being underlined anyway.

Among possible alternatives is the placing of some other diacritic by the voiced consonant, either above or below, or before
or after. The position below tends to be obliterated by underlining, and the position above, though suitable for *s c p*, is
awkward for the tall letters *k t*. Perhaps the best of these is the

acute accent (if available), which is fairly visible and does not obliterate much of the letter; *e.g.*

ကျောင်းသားထူကြီးထဲက

caun:tha:htu.ci:hte:ka.

Alternatively one could use a comma before the voiced consonant, or a raised comma after it; *e.g.*

caun:,tha:,htu.,ci:,hte:,ka.   *caun:th'a:ht'u.c'i:ht'e:k'a.*

A different approach would be to use spacing but avoid the sense-group difficulty by having some convention (say "+) to show that a consonant is not voiced in spite of being joined to the preceding syllable; *e.g.*

လုံခြုံရေး ကော်မီတီ

loun-"hcoun-yei: ko-mi-"ti

Voicing occurring before the weak vowel /ä/ is a different matter. When the words /hka:/ "waist" and /pa'/ "go round" are joined to form the compound word meaning "belt", the first syllable is weakened and one hears sometimes /hkäba'/, sometimes /käba'/, and sometimes /gäba'/, depending on the habits of the speaker and the speed at which he is speaking. To maintain consistency in such cases the simplest procedure is to show the unvoiced sound in the romanization:

ခါးပတ်   ထန်းပင်   တကောင်   ကြမ်းပိုး

/hkäba'/   /htäbin/   /tägaun/   /cäbou:/   etc.

(12) *Spacing*

Most IPA systems separate each syllable from the next by space, which avoids ambiguities between the final of one syllable and the initial of the next, but it is not easy to read. Spacing by sense-groups on the other hand not only falls foul of the final/initial ambiguity problem—*e.g.*

conventional *äthinokäw* could be

either   အသင် ၌ကြော   or   အသိ ၌ကော

      /äthin-ou'o:/   /äthi-nou-ko:/

—but can also lead to long groups of joined syllables which are confusing to the eye; *e.g.*

နိုင်ငံရေး ခေါင်းဆောင်ကြီးများကဲ့သို့

naingganyeigäungzaunggyimyägethọ

Solutions to the problem of syllable division are affected by the choice of tone-marks and other symbols: see the summary below (4.2.3).

4.2.3 Summary

Under current conditions of printing and typing there can be little doubt that if a transcription that can be typewritten without the use of extra diacritics is readable and unambiguous, it will be the most useful for most purposes: if it can be typewritten it can also be printed and written by hand. Cornyn's 1958 transcription fulfills these conditons, and it is therefore recommended here, but with one modification.

The modification concerns the use of *q* for glottal onset. This letter is not required for accuracy (note (7) above) and detracts from the readability of the system. Dispensing with the *q* affects another feature. There are just a few words in which the weak central vowel, transcribed *a* without a tone-mark, is followed by *qi¹, qin, qu¹, qun;* e.g.

ကအင်္ဂ   *taqin-ga*   "one set (of 12 sheets of a palm-leaf manuscript)"

မအိ   *maqi¹*   "not squeeze"

If the *q* is not used these words will be written

tain-ga   >   တုိင်ကာ   "reaching"

mai¹   >   မိုက်   "be stupid"

To separate the two letters *a* and *i* by a hyphen is of course impossible as that would mark *a* as in the "level" tone.

Probably the best way out of this difficulty is to mark the weak vowel in some way. In printing one can use *ă*, but in typing some device such as *a* surmounted by ⚓ seems suitable. The two words above could then be written unambiguously as *täin-ga* and *mäi¹*. In typing, this convention has the slight disadvantage that it requires backspacing, which is not necessary in Cornyn's system; but backspacing is not so formidable an obstacle—typists do it in English for underlining "*e.g.*", "*i.e.*" and so on—and it seems a price worth paying to be rid of the *q*. In fact, since the ambiguity only arises in the few cases where the weak vowel precedes /i/ or /u/ in closed syllables, it would be quite satisfactory to omit the diacritic ⁺ everywhere but in those cases. It might also be desirable to use it in lists of phonemes, etc.; *e.g.* "the vowels /i, a, u, ä/."

Cornyn's mark for "level" tone is a hyphen within a syllable group, but ∅ at the end of a syllable group. It may be objected to this that the use of two marks (- and ∅) is inconsistent and sometimes confusing, at least to beginners; and that, as there are three tones to be marked, it would be more economical to mark two and leave the third unmarked, *i.e.* abolish the hyphen. This would in fact not be possible without altering other features of the system. Besides marking "level" tone, the hyphen serves to distinguish sequences which would be ambiguous without it: final nasal (*n*) followed immediately by *g, y,* or *w* would be ambiguous with initial *ng, ny,* and *nw*. The abolition of the hyphen therefore would necessitate the adoption of an extra symbol for the nasal final (such as the *ñ* of Okell's system), which is hardly worth the gain.

Cornyn's other two tone-marks (+. and +:) are ambiguous in embedded words with English punctuation marks, and there is perhaps a case for replacing them with accents (say ⁺ and ⁺ respectively) or raised commas (⁺' and ⁺"). Accents however are not normally available on English typewriters, and would be uneconomical because some other way would have to be devised for separating syllables which are separated in Cornyn by his dots. The use of raised commas again is marginally ambiguous with quotation marks and would necessitate the use of some other symbol (perhaps *q*) for the final glottal stop. Finally the ambiguity of the dots can be avoided by using oblique strokes (/. . ./), so the case for replacing them is not strong.

It may be desirable for some purposes to mark voicing (note (1.1) above). For this purpose underlining is perhaps the best of an unattractive set of alternatives: there is no need to underline whole words if they are written between oblique strokes. The irregular voicing often heard before the weak vowel /ä/, however, is best left not shown.

Apart from Cornyn, the other transcription system that has much to recommend it is that of the Library of Congress, which, while fairly easy to type, is much closer in appearance than Cornyn to the traditional "Government" transcription of names, etc. It has some small defects. First, there is no provision for avoiding final/initial ambiguities by separating syllables: this can easily be rectified by using hyphens for all syllables within a group; *e.g.*

လက်ဝဲ   *let-wē*   not   *le-twē*

လုပ်အား:   *lok-ā*   not   *lo-kā*

Secondly, there is no separate symbol for the weak vowel: if hyphens are used, as suggested above, this vowel can be shown by *a* without a hyphen; *e.g.*

ငါးသလောက်   *ngathalauk*

This does of course leave unsolved the problem of words like

တအာ့ဆီ   ဗအာ့

but they are not frequent, and a transcription such as this is not likely to be used in contexts where complete overall accuracy is essential.

The tone-marks of the Library of Congress system ($\emptyset$ ς $\bar{\tau}$) are open to objection: they are not available on ordinary typewriters, they look clumsy, and the subscript dot is apt to be obliterated by underlining. The second and third points could be met by using accents (say $\emptyset$ $\acute{\tau}$ $\acute{\tau}$), but this still leaves the problem of availability. The kind of uses to which this system is likely to be put (names of people and places, book titles, etc.) make Cornyn's stop and colon unsuitable, entailing as they do the use of oblique strokes before and after each word or group of words in order to avoid ambiguity with English punctuation. On the other hand, $+$ and $\bar{\tau}$ are used in transliteration, and any typewriter having these two symbols could be used to type words in both methods of romanization. Failing either pair of diacritics, perhaps the best available alternative would be to use the single and double raised commas ($+'$ $+''$) in place of the subscript dot and the overline ($+$ $\bar{\tau}$).

Briefly, the amendments suggested above are:

Cornyn 1958:
   omit *q-*
   use *ä* for the weak vowel, either throughout or only where necessary
   use /. . ./ for embedded words
   use underlining to mark voicing if required

4.2.3

Library of Congress:

hyphenate joined syllables
use *a* without hyphen for the weak vowel
use +́ . +̀ (or +' +") instead of +̣ +̄ if available or preferred

The main differences between the two systems then are:

Cornyn (amended);	*c hc j*	; +' +*n*	; *ä o ou'/oun*;	+. +:
L of C (amended);	*ky ch gy*;	+*t* +*n* ; +*k* +*ng*	; *a aw ok/on* ;	+̣ +̄

These two systems, with the suggested amendments, are recommended for certain purposes in Section 5. They are set out in full in Table 5 (Section 7.1.2) and are referred to as "standard phonetic transcription" and "standard conventional transcription" respectively. Recommended variations for particular requirements are:

phonetic transcription with voicing marked
conventional transcription with accented tones
conventional transcription with raised comma tones

Two short examples are given below to illustrate the use of these systems: a passage of spoken Burmese for the phonetic transcription, and a list of book-titles for the conventional transcription.

Script	*Phonetic transcription* *standard*	*with voicing marked*
ရောင်နီလာလှပေါ့	/Yaun-ni-la-hla.bo.	/Yaun-ni-la-hla.p̱o.
ဆိုတာ ဘာလဲ	hsou-da ba-le:	hsou-ṯa ba-le:
ဆရာမ။	hsäya-ma.	hsäya-ma.
ကိုကိုက ပြောတော့	Kou-kou-ga. pyo:do.	Kou-kou-ḵa. pyo:ṯo.
မိုးလင်းခါ နီးရင်	mou:lin:ga ni:yin	mou:lin:hḵa ni:yin
ကောင်းကင်က	kaun:gin-ga.	kaun:ḵin-ḵa.
နီလာတယ်တဲ့။	ni-la-de-de.	ni-la-ṯe-ṯe.
ကောင်းကင် ဆိုတာ	Kaun:gin hsou-da	Kaun:ḵin hsou-ṯa
ဘာလဲ၊	ba-le:	ba-le:
နီတာ ဆိုတာ	Ni-da hsou-da	Ni-ṯa hsou-ṯa
ဘာလဲ ဟင်။	ba-le:hin/	ba-le:hin/

from: ကြေးမုံ ရိပ်သွင် by ခင်နှင်းယု
ငွေတာရီ၊ ရန်ကုန်၊ ၁၉၆၀။ p.35

Script	Conventional transcription: standard
‌	Taung-ngu-hso yadụ-ahpyei
‌	Sabụ-di-pạ ok-hsāung kyān
‌	Shēi-hāung let-hmụ
‌	pyin-nya-bāung-gyok kyān
‌	That-htụ ru-pakạ wị-la-thani kyān
‌	Min-nān-zi ēi-gyin
‌	thōn-zaung-dwē
‌	Wun-nạ bāw-danạ that-īn

With accented tones	With raised comma tones
Taung-ngu-hsou yadú-ahpyei	Taung-ngu-hsou yaduⁱahpyei
Sabú-di-pá ok-hsaùng kyàn	Sabuⁱdi-paⁱ ok-hsaungⁱⁱ kyanⁱⁱ
Sheì-haùng let-hmú	Shei ⁱⁱhaungⁱⁱ let-hmuⁱ
pyin-nya-baùng-gyok kyàn	pyin-nya-baungⁱⁱgyok kyanⁱⁱ
That-htú ru-paká	That-htuⁱ ru-pakaⁱ
wí-la-thani kyàn	wiⁱla-thani kyanⁱⁱ
Min-nàn-zi eì-gyìn	Minⁱⁱnanⁱⁱzi eiⁱⁱgyinⁱⁱ
thòn-zaung-dwè	thonⁱⁱzaung-dweⁱⁱ
Wun-ná bàw-daná that-ìn	Wun-naⁱ bawⁱⁱdanaⁱ that-inⁱⁱ

from: List of text publications
  in Journal of the Burma Research Society 49 (1966); p.248

4.3 Combined method

The system set out below as representative of the combined method is that of Minn Latt 1966. As a combined system is designed to represent both the symbols and the sounds of Burmese, it is set out below first against the script, then against the phonemes.

Minn Latt's 1966 system is used by Bečková (1967), and is almost the same as that used by Minn Latt in 1958 and 1962–64. The difference is that his earlier *th sh š θ* later became *ht hs sh th*.

The only other combined system is the unpublished and not quite complete one devised by Becker c.1965. Variants from Minn Latt 1966 are shown in the notes.

4.3.1

4.3.1 Table 3a: Minn Latt's system with Burmese script

Consonants

Scr က ခ ဂ ဃ င စ ဆ ဇ ဈ ည ဋ ဌ ဍ ဎ ဏ တ

ML	k	kh	g	gh	ng	s	hs	z	zh	nj	nj	ṭ	ht	ḍ	dh	ṇ	t
	t(1)	c(1)	d		n(1)	(2)				(9)	(4)		(2)				
		(2)	(1)														

Scr ထ ဒ ဓ န ပ ဖ ဗ ဘ မ ယ ရ လ ၀ သ ဟ ဠ အ

ML	ht	d	dh	n	p	ph	b	bh	m	j	y	l	w	th	h	ḷ	(a)
	(2)					(2)				ṣ	s(5)						(6)
											r						

Finals (9)

Vowels (7)

Scr + +ာ/ါ ိ ီ ုႆ/+ု ုုႆ/+ုု ေ+ ဲ ေ+ာ/ါ ေ+ာ်/ော် ို

    − − ကျ ကြ ကု ကူ ၀ − ဩ ကော် −

ML	a	á	i	í	u	ú	éi	ə	ô	ó	óu
	ă										
	ā										

Finals (9)

Scr +က် ေ+ာက် ုိက် +စ် − +တ် ုတ် ိတ် ေတ် +ပ် ုပ် ိပ် ုပ် −

ML ek   auk   aik   is   at   ut   eit   out   ap   up   eip   oup

Scr +င် ေ+ာင် ုိင် +ဉ် +ည် +န် ုန် ိန် ေန် ံ ုံ ိံ ုံ +ယ်

ML in   aun   ain   in   ij   an   un   ein   oun   am   um   eim   oum   é
                          (8)   (8)

Medials	Tone marks (10)	Punctuation	Figures
Scr ျ ြ ွ ှ	+etc. +etc. +: etc.	၊ ။	၁၂၃၄၅၆၇၈၉၀
ML ⌠+j +y+ w h+	↓ + ^	as for Eng.	1234567890
(5) +u	by pronunciation		
(8)			

Abbreviations: in full (e.g. ၌ hnaik, ၍ ywei) but ၏ i

Spacing (11): leave space between expressions, between a word and its grammatical suffixes, and elsewhere at discretion

4.3.1 Table 3b: Minn Latt's system with Burmese sounds in standard phonetic transcription

Initials:

plosives etc.: aspirate (2)	plain	voiced (3)	
Std /hk ht hp hc hs/	/k t p c s th/	/g d b j z dh/	
ML ⎰ *kh ht ph cj hs*	*k t p tj s th*	*g d, dh b dj z --*	
⎱ *ht cy*	*t̠ ty*	*gh d̠, dh bh dy zh*	
(1)	(1)	(1) (1)	(1) (1)

nasals etc.: aspirate	plain	others
Std /hng hn hm hny hl sh hw/	/ng n m ny l y w/	/r h/
ML ⎰ *hng hn hm hnj hl sh hw*	*ng n m nj l j w*	*r h* (6)
⎱ *hnj̠ sh̠*	*nj̠ l̠ y*	
hny	*ny*	
(1) (1) (5)	(1) (1) (5)	
	(4)	

Vowels (7): open syllables	closed syllables
Std /i ei e a o ou u ä̈/	/i ei ai a au ou u e/
ML ⎰ *i ei e a o ou u (ä̆)*	*i ei ai a au ou u e*
⎱ *ij ij̠ ij*	
(9) (9) (9)	(8)

Medials	Finals (9)		Tones (10)	Voicing (11)
Std /y w/	/+ˈ	+ n/	/+(-) + +:/	write in voiced phoneme
ML ⎰ *j w*	*+k*	*+ng*	*₣ + ₴*	write unvoiced phoneme
⎱ *y*	*+t*	*+n*		without preceding space
	+p	*+m*		(with some exceptions)
	+s	*+n̠*		
(5)	etc	etc		

Spacing (11)

Std syllables joined, with hyphens where necessary; sense-groups spaced

ML leave space between expressions, between a word and its grammatical suffixes, and elsewhere at discretion

4.3.2 Combined method: notes and variants

(1) က ခ ဂ င ငှ > *k kh g ng hng*

ကျ ချ ဂျ > *tj cj dj*

ကြ ခြ ဂြ ငြ ငြှ > *ty cy dy ny hny*

In changing in this way from *k* to *t* and *c*, from *g* to *d*, and from *ng* to *n*, Minn Latt hardly gains in plausibility what he loses in correspondence with the script. He might have done better to write

kj khj gj
ky khy gy ngy

—a convention which has the added advantage of being closer to the familiar Government system.

Becker keeps *r* for the second medial, and so writes

ky khy gy
kr khr gr ngr

(2) ခ ဌ ထ ဖ ဆ > *kh ḥt ht ph hs*

Minn Latt prefers to write the *h* of his aspirate plosives etc. after the other letter, but is obliged to write it before in the case of *ht ḥt hs* in order to keep *sh th* for representing fricatives. In his 1958 system he used *hs θ* for these two and so was able to keep the aspirates consistent: *kh th ṭh ph sh.*

Becker, with an eye on library cataloguing, writes *k*ˡ *ṭ*ˡ *t*ˡ *p*ˡ *s*ˡ for this set, and, consistently, *g*ˡ *ḍ*ˡ *d*ˡ *b*ˡ *z*ˡ for the "voiced" set.

(3) *Voiced plosives, etc.*

For words pronounced with a voiced initial consonant but usually spelt with the plain or aspirate equivalent, such as

ခွေ	ချိုး	ထောက်	ချိတ်	ပုံ
"hoop"	"dove"	"spoke"	"hook"	"drum"

Minn Latt prefers to write the voiced form but leaves the alternative to individual preference.

(4) ည ဉ > *nj ṇj*

Becker uses *ṅ* for the first of these—oddly, since this symbolization is widely used for the velar nasal—and has no separate symbol for the second.

For Minn Latt's conventions for these letters as final consonants see note (9).

(5) ဃ ရ > *j y/r*

ယ ၛ > *j y*

ꩻ ၦ > *ṣh sh*

Minn Latt uses his alternative *r* when the pronunciation requires it. Becker keeps to *r* throughout, which is consistent but gives many implausible renderings. For Minn Latt's *ṣh sh* Becker has *ṣ̌ ṣ̌*.

(6) *Glottal onset*

Unlike some of the IPA-type transcription systems, neither Minn Latt nor Becker use a symbol for glottal onset.

(7) *Vowels*

The weak vowel (/ä/), which has no special symbolization in Burmese script, is not shown by Becker: he simply writes whatever vowel symbols occur in the script; *e.g.*

သ ခင်   ဘူ ရင်

thạ kʰing   bʰụ ring
Minn Latt does the same—*e.g.*

စစ်ကိုင်း ကူတို

siskâin kûtou (=/sägain kädou./)
—except that when the weak vowel is spelt, as it most often is, with ∅ vowel symbol, he writes *ắ*; *e.g.*

ကပြား   ကချ

kapyâ but   *kăbja*

For the remaining vowels Becker uses the same conventions as Minn Latt except that in open syllables

for Minn Latt's *ei o ou*
he has   *ej aw o*

(8) ၃ဉ် etc. > *ut etc.*

Minn Latt writes *u* and *wu* for the script's medial and initial *w* when the pronunciation requires it:

၃ဉ်	၃ဉ်	၃ဉ်	၃		ဝဉ်	ဝဉ်	ဝဉ်	ဝ
ut	*un*	*up*	*uṃ*		*wut*	*wun*	*wup*	*wuṃ*

49

4.3.2

Becker keeps closer to transliteration with
wat   wan   wap   wan (sic)

(9) *Finals*

For irregular finals Minn Latt uses ad hoc conventions; *e.g.*

ကိုယ်   စိုလ်   မဂ်   သုံး:   ဥယျာဉ်   လိင်   ခေတ်
kóuj   bóul   meg   thôuṇ   ujjiṇ   léing   khit

He does not distinguish consecutive final-initial pairs of consonants from conjunct consonants.

Becker's finals agree with Minn Latt's with the following exceptions:

for Minn Latt's   *is   in   aṃ   ouṃ   ij   iṇ*
Becker has   *iˡ   ing   an   oun   iṅ   iṅ*

Minn Latt's conventions for +ည် do not take account of its alternative pronunciations: /*i   ei   e*/. He might with advantage have rendered these *ij   eij   ej*.

(10) *Tones*

For Minn Latt's   ⌁   +   ⌁

Becker has   +   ṭ   +:

Induced creaky tone in a level tone syllable is shown in Minn Latt by a subscript dot:

သူ   ›   *thú*

but it seems to be ignored in a heavy tone syllable such as

သန်:   in   ခင်သန်:ဆီ

Becker marks it in the latter case by using two tone-marks: *thaṇ:*, but cannot show it in level tone syllables as he has no separate mark for them.

(11) *Voicing and spacing*

Becker does not show voicing at all, and leaves space between each syllable, which makes his romanization difficult to read; *e.g.*

အတိတေ ကလ ရှေ: မဆွ   အခါ
a ti tej ka la šej: ma sˡwa ạ kˡa

Minn Latt uses spacing to show voicing up to a point: as it "can create extremely long sequences of syllables" he proposes the following principles to help break them up.

"1. No word, or highword, contains any space inside it. This also applies to words of foreign origin like *hóté*.
2. Grammatical words [suffixes] stand apart from the lexical words they modify. . . .
3. . . . Consecutive grammatical words may be combined arbitrarily in groups not containing more than three syllables each."

The following is an extract from his example:
Améirikán Pyíjhtáunsu ka lóulâ thíj hu, Du thămăta Hámphărêi ka pyô hsóu thíj
In view of the difficulty of delimiting "words" in Burmese, the elasticity of Minn Latt's suggestions is welcome, but it seems a pity to separate suffixes from the words to which they are attached. There are not often more than three, and confusingly long sequences can easily be divided by hyphens.

4.3.3 Summary

Minn Latt's combined system, with its use of *ă* and *ut* etc., gives more weight to pronunciation than Becker's, but it has some serious defects in this respect. A number of words in this romanization can hardly be described as plausible; *e.g.*

ရှ	ပုဒ်	ပြည်
/hca./	/pou¹/	/pyei/
cja	poud	pyij

There is also the failure to write in voicing; *e.g.*

ပြည်ထောင်စုက	ရန်ကုန်ကို ဆင်းသွားတော့
/pyei-daun-zu.ga./	/yan-goun-gou hsin:dhwa:do./
pyíjhtáunsu ka	Yánkóun kóu hsînthwâ to

and the failure to show weakening (except when spelt with Ø vowel symbol in the script); *e.g.*

အဏ္ဍာ	ဘူရာ:	ထား:ပြ
/bäda/	/hpäya:/	/dämya./
bhaṇḍá	bhuyâ	htâpya

Minn Latt's system also needs some device to avoid final/initial ambiguities; *e.g.*

his *înwa* *pănjámjâ* *tjatja*
could be အင်းဝ ပညာများ ကျကျ
or အီးန္ဝ ပညာမ်ယား ကျတ်ယ

Both Becker's and Minn Latt's systems might have been more satisfactory if they had adopted a plausible and consistent transcription as a basis and then employed diacritics to reveal the spelling. Such a system would not be able to cope with very irregular spellings any better than Minn Latt's, and it would need more diacritics than his four (+̌ +̂ +́ +̣'), but at least it would give a more consistent indication of pronunciation.

Suppose, for example, the transcription represented nasal final by + *n*, then the six common ways of spelling this in Burmese script could be indicated by diacritics in some such way as this:

င် ဉ် ဏ် န် မ် +ံ
ṅ ñ ṇ n n̄ ń

If the stop final were transcribed as +*q* its five common spellings could be indicated in the same way:

က် စ် ဋ် တ် ပ်
q̇ q̃ q̣ q q̄

Probably some economies could be effected here, since the distribution of letters is such that, for example, the stop in the rhymes /e' ai' au'/ is not normally spelt with any other letter than the first.

Voicing could be written in, and a diacritic (say +̊) used to show that a voiced phoneme is written with an unvoiced letter, and vice versa; *e.g.*

ရန်ကုန် ခေါင်း နောက်ဘေး
yan-g̊oun *g̊haun:* *nauq̊-hp̊ei:*

Another diacritic (say +̣) could be used to show "rhotacization"; *e.g.*

ယှက် ရှက် ကျ ကြ ပီ ပြီ ပထမ ပဌမ
sheq̇ ṣheq̇ *ca. c̣a.* *pi p̣i* *păhtăma.* *păhṭăma.*

Another diacritic (say +̃) could be used for "palatalization"; *e.g.*

ဣ +ည် ေ+ +ည် +ယ်+ည် ပျစ် ပစ်
i ĩ *ei eĩ* *e ẽ* *pyiq* *pỹiq*

If it were made clear that the mark of a weak syllable (say ˘)
overrides other signs, the spelling of many weak syllables could
be shown, *e.g.*

ဘူရာː   ကူːတို့   ကုလာːထိုင်

hpŭ.ya: *kŭ:dou.*   *kŭ.lă:htaiṅ*

Weak syllables written with a final consonant are more difficult:
one might perhaps resort to small raised letters or brackets; *e.g.*

မန့်ကျည်ː   ပန်ːပူ   ထမင်ːရည်   နှစ်ယောက်

mă'ñi: *pă'ⁿbu.*   *htămiⁿyeī*   *hniꟼyauḋ*

mă(n)ñĩ   *pă(n:)bu.*   *htămĭ(ṅ:)yeī*   *hnĭ(ꟼ)yauḋ*

Whatever particular conventions were adopted for a system on
these principles, at least the phonemes of Burmese would be
given a fairly consistent symbolization. The idea is not pursued
here at length since the result would no doubt be unusably
cumbersome, despite its advantages in other respects; further-
more, the combined method altogether is discarded as less
informative and less practical than either transcription or transliteration, or both.

5   CONCLUSION: CHOICE OF SYSTEM

The preceding Sections have shown something of the wide variety of existing romanization systems for Burmese, and have pointed to some further possibilities. Any potential user must choose one of the existing systems or devise a new one for himself. His choice will be guided by three main considerations: why he wants a romanization at all, what it should be able to do, and what makes one convention preferable to another.

It is worth bearing in mind that the primary reason for using a romanization is because one is writing for readers who do not know the script, or because one does not have access to typists and printers who can reproduce it. There are therefore occasions when a romanization is not necessary at all, even for books and articles written in roman-script languages—*e.g.* articles in English in the Journal of the Burma Research Society.

If a romanization is found to be necessary, one turns to the second consideration. Nearly all potential users can be placed in one of three categories, each of which has different demands to make of a romanization. The categories may be called "literary", "linguistic", and "casual".

In the literary group are literary historians, who need to quote from texts old and new; epigraphists, who want the romanization to reproduce each of the symbols they have found on an inscription; scholars of Buddhism, who want the names of texts, persons and concepts to be written in the form used by scholars outside Burma; and comparative linguists who believe that the spelling of a word may hold clues to the form it had at an earlier stage of development of the language. All these persons are concerned with the written form of Burmese words, not with its current pronunciation, and for them therefore the transliteration method has obvious attractions.

The linguistic group includes teachers and learners of spoken Burmese, phoneticians and general linguists. For them the sounds of the language are more important than the written forms, so they need an accurate transcription method, as close to the IPA type as they desire or can afford.

The third category, the casual users, includes anthropologists, political scientists, economists, geographers, librarians, journalists and traders. Their need is to refer simply and unambiguously to people and places, and to products and occasional concepts for which there is no accurate equivalent in their own language. For their purposes the Government system of transcription, since it is what has mostly been used in writings of this kind, would be suitable if it were not so inconsistent. If they wish to be consistent and fairly accurate they will choose something akin to one of the conventional types of transcription.

It would be ideal if all these needs could be met by a single system, but the difficulty of achieving this has been described above (Section 4.3.3). The combined method is perhaps the furthest one can go towards the ideal, but it is a compromise, entailing substantial sacrifices. It is hardly detailed enough for such purposes as epigraphy and comparative linguistics, nor does it conform to the internationally used romanization of Pali; it is not easy to see how it could be informative or clear enough for language work; and it differs too greatly from the traditional "conventional" transcriptions to be attractive to casual users. The conclusion is then that one must choose between transliteration or transcription according to one's needs, sometimes giving both forms if necessary.

Once the method has been chosen, one comes to the third consideration, about what constitutes a good system. The user's choice here depends on how far a given system can meet the conflicting requirements enumerated in Section 4: that it should be unambiguous, plausible, easily memorized, readable, economical, readily available, and traditional. People have their own predilections in these matters, but it is suggested that the three systems recommended above (in Sections 4.1.3, 4.2.3) will be found satisfactory for different purposes:

standard transliteration   for "literary" work
phonetic transcription   for "linguistic" work
conventional transcription   for "casual" work

These three systems are set out in full in Tables 4 and 5 (Section 7.1).

Writers who make use of them will want to indicate which of the three they are using, and in order to save cumbersome identifications (particularly in texts where some words are transliterated and others transcribed), they can be distinguished typographically as follows:

standard transliteration in *italics* (or underlined in typewriting)
– the usual convention for foreign words
phonetic transcription in /oblique strokes/
– the usual convention in linguistic work
conventional transcription in plain type
– since it may mostly be used for the names of people and places embedded in an English or other language text; booktitles however could be italicized/underlined as usual.

For example:

"Ū Hlạ Thēin explains in his article 'Mwēi-zā Sagalōn-my how the word for lon-gyi derives from Persian *lungi*. Pronounced /loun-ji/ in modern Burmese, it has become so well established that many writers spell it *lum-khyaññ* thinking it is a compound of /loun/ 'to be covered' and /hci/ 'to tie up'."

It is hoped that the three systems recommended here will find favour and so promote a reduction in the number and variety of systems in current use. It need hardly be said that this cannot be the last word on the subject: the expanding world of Burmese studies can look forward to new arguments and fresh ideas which will improve the present unsatisfactory situation.

6 BIBLIOGRAPHY

Allott, A. J.
Categories for the description of the verbal syntagma in Burmese
in Lingua 15 pp. 283–309; 1965

Grammatical tone in modern spoken Burmese
in Wissenschaftliche Zeitschrift der Karl-Marx-Universität Leipzig 16 pp. 157–161; 1967

Armstrong, Lilias E., and Pe Maung Tin
A Burmese phonetic reader
University of London Press, London; 1925

Ba Shin
Lokahteikpan
Burma Historical Commission, Rangoon; 1962

Ballard, Emilie
Lessons in spoken Burmese, book 1
Burma Baptist Convention, Rangoon; 1961

Becker, A. L.
Burmese transliteration
Typescript; c.1965

Bečková, Dagmar
A few notes on Theippám Máun Wa's semi-fictional works
in Archiv Orientální 35 pp. 95–110; 1967

Bernot, Denise
Esquisse d'une description phonologique du birman
in Bulletin de la Société Linguistique de Paris 58 pp. 164–224; 1963

Le vocabulaire concret du Birman et les notions abstraites
in Revue de l'école nationale des langues orientales vol.3 pp.1–18; 1966

The vowel systems of Arakanese and Tavoyan
in Lingua 15 pp. 463–474; 1965

6

Blagden, C. O.
The transliteration of Old Burmese inscriptions
in Journal of the Burma Research Society 4 pp. 136–139;
1914
Bridges, J. E.
Burmese grammar
British Burma Press, Rangoon, 1915

——— Burmese petitions, letters and other papers transliterated
Bridges, London; 1908

——— Burmese stories and other papers: transliteration and notes
Bridges, London; n.d.

——— Burmese manual
Luzac, London, and British Burma Press, Rangoon; 1906
Butwell, R.
U Nu of Burma
Stanford University Press; 1963
Cornyn, W. S.
Outline of Burmese grammar
in Language 20 (supplement: language dissertation 38); 1944

——— Spoken Burmese: books 1 and 2
Henry Holt; 1945
——— and J. K. Musgrave
Burmese Glossary (American Council of Learned Societies'
Program in Oriental Languages: Publication Series A:
Texts: No.5)
American Council of Learned Societies, New York; 1958
——— and D. Haigh Roop
Beginning Burmese
Yale University Press, New Haven & London; 1968

Crawfurd, J.
Journal of an embassy . . . to the court of Ava
Colburn, London; 1834
Duroiselle, C.
Epigraphia birmanica vol. 1 part 1
Government Printing, Rangoon; 1919

Burmese philology
in Journal of the Burma Research Society 3 pp. 13–21; 1913

Literal transliteration of the Burmese alphabet
in Journal of the Burma Research Society 6 pp. 81–90; 1916
Firth, J. R.
Notes on the transcription of Burmese
in Bulletin of the School of Oriental Studies 7 pp. 137–140; 1933

Alphabets and phonology in India and Burma
in Bulletin of the School of Oriental Studies 8 pp. 517–541; 1936
Grant Brown, R.
Half the battle in Burmese
Oxford University Press, London; 1910

The international phonetic association
in Journal of the Burma Research Society 2 pp. 57–61; 1912
Haas, Mary
The use of numeral classifiers in Burmese
in Semitic and oriental studies (University of California Publications in Semitic Philology No.11)
University of California, Berkeley-Los Angeles; 1951
Hla Pe
A re-examination of Burmese "classifiers"
in Lingua 15 pp. 163–185; 1965

The origin and development of the Burmese composite word
Mô Kwan:
in Bulletin of the School of Oriental and African Studies 13 pp. 427–432; 1950
Hunter, W. W.
Guide to the orthography of Indian proper names with a list showing the true spelling of all post towns and villages in India
Government Printing, Calcutta; 1871

6

Imperial gazetteer of India
Trübner, London; 1881

Jones, R. B., and U Khin
The Burmese writing system (American Council of Learned
Societies' Program in Oriental Languages: Publications
Series B: Aids: No.1)
American Council of Learned Societies, Washington; 1953

Latter, T.
Grammar of the language of Burmah
Ostell Lepage et al., Calcutta and London; 1845

Luce, G. H.
Names of the Pyu
in Journal of the Burma Research Society 22 p. 90; 1932

McDavid, R. I.
Burmese phonemics
in Studies in Linguistics 3 pp. 6–18; 1945

Minn Latt
The Prague method romanization of Burmese
in Archiv Orientální 26 pp. 145–167; 1958

Mainstreams in Burmese Literature
in New Orient Bimonthly 1960/1 pp. 13–16, 1960/3
pp. 23–25, 1960/6 pp. 5–8, 1961/6 pp. 172–175, 1962/6
pp. 172–176

Reports on studies in Burmese grammar
in Archiv Orientální 30 pp. 49–115 (first report); 1962
                        31 pp. 230–273 (second report); 1963
                        32 pp. 265–292 (third report); 1964
————(Mînn Latt Yêkháun)
Modernization of Burmese (dissertationes orientales vol. 11)
Oriental Institute, Prague; 1966

Nash, Manning
The golden road to modernity: village life in contemporary
Burma
Wiley, New York; 1965

Okell, John
A reference grammar of colloquial Burmese
Oxford University Press, London; 1969

Nissaya Burmese: a case of systematic adaptation to a foreign grammar and syntax
in Lingua 15 pp. 186–227; 1965
Pemberton, R. B.
Journey from Munipoor to Ava (1830; ed. D. G. E. Hall)
in Journal of the Burma Research Society 43 pp. 1–96; 1960
St Barbe, H. L.
Burmese transliteration
in Journal of the Royal Asiatic Society 10 pp. 228–233; 1878
St John, R. F. St A.
Burmese self-taught
Marlborough, London; n.d. [6th impression early 1960s]
Sprigg, R. K.
Junction in spoken Burmese
in Studies in linguistic analysis (Philological Society Publication) pp. 104–138
Blackwell, Oxford; 1957

Comparison of Arakanese and Burmese based on phonological formulae
in Linguistic comparison in South East Asia and the Pacific (ed. H. Shorto) pp. 109–132
School of Oriental and African Studies, London; 1963

Prosodic analysis and phonological formulae in Tibeto–Burman linguistic comparison
in Linguistic comparison in South East Asia and the Pacific (ed. H. Shorto) pp. 79–108
School of Oriental and African Studies, London; 1963

Burmese orthography and the tonal classification of Burmese lexical items
in Journal of the Burma Research Society 47 pp. 415–440; 1964

Prosodic analysis and Burmese syllable-initial features in Anthropological linguistics 7/6 pp. 59–81; 1965

Stewart, J. A.
Introduction to colloquial Burmese
British Burma Press, Rangoon; 1936

———
Manual of colloquial Burmese
Luzac, London; 1955
——— and others
A Burmese English dictionary: parts 1–5 (in progress)
Luzac, London, and others; 1940–

Taw Sein Ko
Elementary handbook of the Burmese language
American Baptist Mission Press, Rangoon; 1898 (2nd ed. 1913)

Symes, M.
An account of an embassy to the kingdom of Ava
Nicol and Wright, London; 1800

Than Tun
Religion in Burma
in Journal of the Burma Research Society 42 pp. 47–69; 1959

Whitbread, K.
Catalogue of Burmese books in the India Office Library
1969

Yi Yi
The thrones of the Burmese kings
In Journal of the Burma Research Society 43 pp. 95–123; 1960

Yule, H.
Narrative of the mission . . . to the court of Ava
Smith Elder, London; 1858

[Government of Burma]
Tables for the transliteration of Burmese into English
Government Printing, Rangoon; 1883, 1890, 1907, 1930

[Library of Congress]
Cataloging service bulletin 76
Library of Congress, Washington D.C.; 1966

In Burmese:

Shwei Thwin
  That-dá-bei-dá achei-gan
  in Tet-gatho-pyin-nya-padei-tha sa-zaung 1 pp. 231–242; 1966

7 REFERENCE TABLES

7.1 Recommended systems

7.1.1 Table 4: Standard transliteration

Consonants

Scr	က	ခ	ဂ	ဃ	င	စ	ဆ	ဇ	ဈ	ည	ဋ	ဌ	ဍ	ဎ	ဏ	တ
Std	k	kh	g	gh	ṅ	c	ch	j	jh	ññ	ñ	ṭ	ṭh	ḍ	ḍh	ṇ	t

Scr	ထ	ဒ	ဓ	န	ပ	ဖ	ဗ	ဘ	မ	ယ	ရ	လ	ဝ	သ	ဟ	ဠ	အ
Std	th	d	dh	n	p	ph	b	bh	m	y	r	l	w	s	h	ḷ	ʼ+

Vowels

Scr	+	+ɔ/ါ	ိ	ီ	ု/ှ	ူ/ှ	ေ+	ဲ	ေ+ɔ/	ေ+ɔ/ ᵒ	ုᵒ
Std	a	ā	i	ī	u	ū	e	ai	o	ō	ui

Finals

Scr	ံ	်᷇

Std ṁ   shown by following space or tone-mark or ʼ+ or hyphen

Medials				Tone marks		Punctuation		Figures
Scr	ျ	ြ	ွ	ှ	့	း	၊	။	၁၂၃၄၅၆၇၈၉၀
Std	y	r	w	h	+.	+:	/	//	1234567890

Abbreviations: in full (starred if desired); ၏ gives eʹ (or *cʹ)

Spacing: syllables joined, with hyphens at discretion; sense-groups spaced

Type: normally italicized in print, underlined in typewriting

Variation: simplified transliteration (requiring only + and ₮)
As standard except that ṅ ṁ ñ > ng ṃ ñ

Note: The following conjunct consonants have special forms.

Scr	င	ည	ည	ဋ	ဍ	ဏ	န	သ
Std	ṅ	jjh	ñjh	ṭṭh	ḍḍh	nth	nd	ss

For the rarely used 'Sanskrit' symbols see 4.1.2 note (13).

7.1.2.

7.1.2 Table 5: Standard phonetic transcription and standard conventional transcription with script equivalents

Common Burmese script equivalents (B) are given to aid identification; the conventional system (C) is shown only where it differs from the phonetic system (P)

Initials:

Plosives etc.: aspirate	plain	voiced
B ခ ထ ဖ ချ ဆ	က တ ပ ကျ စ သ	ဂ ဒ ဗ ဂျ ဇ –
P /hk ht hp hc hs/	/k t p c s th/	/g d b j z dh/
C ch	ky	gy th

Nasals etc.: aspirate	plain	Others
B ငှ နှ မှ ညှ လှ ရှ ဝှ	င န မ ည လ ယ ဝ	ရ ဟ
P /hng hn hm hny hl sh hw/	/ng n m ny l y w/	/r h /
C		

Vowels: open syllables	Closed syllables
B +ီ ေ+ +ယ် +ာ ေ+ာ် +ို +ူ -	+စ်/ဥ် +ိတ်/+ိန် +ိုက်/+ိုင် +တ်/+န် ေ+ာက်/ေ+ာင် +ုတ်/+ုန် +ွတ်/+ွန် +…
P /i ei e a o ou u ä/ or/ a/	/i ei ai a au ou u e/
C aw o a	o
conventional finals:	t/n k/n k/ng t/n k/ng k/n t/n t

Medials	Finals	Tones	Voicing
B +ျ +ွ	+က်/စ် +င်/ဥ် etc. etc.	+ +့ +း etc. etc. etc.	–
P /y w/	/+' +n/	/+(-) +. +:/	write in voiced phoneme
C	+t/k +n/ng	+(-) +̣ +̄	except initial before /ä/

Spacing

B at discretion

P syllables joined, with hyphens where necessary; sense-groups spaced

C

Type

P normally roman type between oblique strokes /. . ./

C normally roman type

Variations:

Phonetic transcription with voicing marked
As standard phonetic except for voicing use the unvoiced
consonant underlined; *e.g.*

script: စဉ်းစားတယ်   မ ဆင်းချင်ဘူး

standard: /sin:za:de/   /mähsin:jin-bu:/

with voicing marked: /sin:s̱a:ṯe/   /mähsin:hçin-hpu:/

Conventional transcription with accented tones
As standard conventional except for ´+ ⊤̣ use ⊹̣ ⊹̣ ; *e.g.*

script: သွား ကြ ပါ အုံး မ ယ် ရှင်

standard: thwā-gya̱-ba-oūn-me-shi̱n

with accented tones: thwà-gyá-ba-oùn-me-shín

Conventional transcription with raised comma tones
As standard conventional except for ⊹̣ ⊤̣ use +' +"; *e.g.*

script and standard: as above

with raised comma tones: thwa" gya' ba-oun" me-shin'

7.2

7.2 Table 6: Major transcriptions in current use

Initials

Plosives etc.:	aspirate					plain						voiced					
Scr	ဗ	ဏ	ဖ	ဈ	ဿ	က	ဘ	ပ	ကျ	၆	သ	ဂ	၃	ဗ	ဂျ	၉	-
Spr	kh	th	ph	ţh	sh	k	t	p	ţ	s	θ	g	d	b	dʐ	z	ð
St	kh	th	ph	ch	sh	k	t	p	c	s	θ	g	d	b	j	z	ð
Cnl	kh	th	ph	ch	sh	k	t	p	c	s	θ	g	d	b	j	z	ð
Cn2	hk	ht	hp	hc	hs	k	t	p	c	s	th	g	d	b	j	z	dh
Ok	hk	ht	hp	hc	hs	k	t	p	c	s	th	g	d	b	j	z	dh
Bal	hk	ht	hp	ch	hs	k	t	p	ty	s	th	g	d	b	j	z	th
LC	hk	ht	hp	ch	hs	k	t	p	ky	s	th	g	d	b	gy	z	th
Gov	k	t	p	ch	s	k	t	p	ky	s	th	g	d	b	gy	z	th
ML ⎰	kh	ht	ph	cj	hs	k	t	p	tj	s	th	g	d/dh	b	dj	z	—
⎱				cy					ty			gh	d/dh	bh	dy	zh	

Nasals etc.:	aspirate							plain							Others		
Scr	၆	၅	၆	ည	လ	၅	၆	င	၆	မ	ည	လ	ဝ	ဝ	ရ	ဟ	-
Spr	ŋ̊	n̥	m̥	ɲ̊	l̥	ɸ	w̥	ŋ	n	m	ɲ	l	j	w	ɾ	h	ʔ
St	hŋ	hn	hm	hny	hl	ʃ	hw	ŋ	n	m	ny	l	y	w	r	h	–
Cnl	hŋ	hn	hm	hny	hl	š	–	ŋ	n	m	ny	l	y	w	r	h	ʔ
Cn2	hng	hn	hm	hny	hl	sh	–	ng	n	m	ny	l	y	w	r	h	q
Ok	hng	hn	hm	hny	hl	hy	hw	ng	n	m	ny	l	y	w	r	h	–
Bal	hng	hn	hm	hny	hl	sh	–	ng	n	m	ny	l	y	w	–	h	–
LC	hng	hn	hm	hny	hl	sh	hw	ng	n	m	ny	l	y	w	r	h	–
Gov	hng	hn	hm	hny	hl	sh	hw	ng	n	m	ny	l	y	w	r	h	–
ML ⎰	hng	hn	hm	hnj	hl	sh	hw	ng	n	m	nj	l	j	w	r	h	–
⎱				hnj̣	ṣh						nj	ḷ	y				
				hny							ny						

68

Vowels:

	Open syllables								Closed syllables							
Scr	ဣ	ဧ+	႟ဲ	+ာ	ဧ+ဲ	ဩ	◌	◌	+ိ	◌	◌	a	au	ou	◌	◌
Spr	i	e	ɛ	a	ɔ	o	u	ə	ι	ei	ai	a	au	ou	o	ɛ
St	i	e	ɛ	a	ɔ	o	u	ə	i	ei	ai	a	au	ou	u	ɛ
Cnl	i	ei	e	a	o	ou	u	a	i	ei	ai	a	au	ou	u	e
Cn2	i	ei	e	a	o	ou	u	a	i	ei	ai	a	au	ou	u	e
Ok	i	ei	e	a	o	ou	u	ă	i	ei	ai	a	au	ou	u	e
Bal	ee	ey	eh	a	aw	o	oo	a	i	ey	ai	a	au	o	u	e
LC	i	ei	e	a	aw	o	u	a	i	ei	ai	a	au	o	u	e
Gov	i	e	è	a	aw	o	u	a	i	ei	ai	a	au	ô	u	e
finals used in LC and Gov:									t/n	k/n	k/ng	t/n	k/ng	k/n	t/n	t
ML {	i	ei	e	a	o	ou	u	(ă)	i	ei	ai	a	au	ou	u	e
	ij	ÿ	ij													

	Medials	Finals		Tones			Voicing	References
Scr	◌ ◌	+က်/◌ etc	+င်/◌ etc	+ ◌ +: etc etc etc			—	
Spr	j w	+ʔ	+̃	- (+') -			write in	Sprigg *Junction* 1957
St	y w	+ʔ	+ŋ	+ +́ +̀			ʔ/̣ or spacing	Stewart *Manual* 1955
Cnl	y w	+ʔ	+n	+̣ +̀ +̂			write in	Cornyn 1 *Outline* 1944
Cn2	y w	+'	+n	+(-) +. +:			write in	Cornyn 2 *Glossary* 1958
Ok	y w	+ʔ	+ñ	+ +̀ +̂			underline	Okell *Grammar* 1969
Bal	y w	+'	+n	+(-)+̣ +:			write in	Ballard *Lessons* 1961
LC	y w	+t/k	+n/ng	+ +̣ +̂			write in	Library of C *Catalog* 1966
Gov	y w	+t/k	+n/ng	- - -			write in	Government *Tables* 1930
ML {	j w	+k/t/p	+ng/n/m	+̂ + +̂			by spacing	Minn Latt *Mod'izat'n* 1966
	y	etc	etc					

Cornyn and Roop's *Beginning Burmese* 1968 = Cn2 but with *hy* for his *sh*
standard phonetic = Cn2 but without his *q−*, and with /ä/ for his weak vowel *a*
standard conventional = LC but with hyphens between joined syllables (except after the weak vowel)

Printed in the United Kingdom
by Lightning Source UK Ltd.
102562UKS00001B/11